RELIEF

a journal of art and faith

spring 2018

www.reliefjournal.com

Editor in Chief	CNF Editor	Lead Editorial
Daniel Bowman Jr.	Jo Anna Gaona	Assistant
		Samantha Hurst
Managing Editor	**Poetry Editor**	
Hannah Haney	John Ballenger	**Editorial Assistants**
		Mary Anleitner
Senior Editor	**Book Review Editor**	Kaylen Dwyer
Brad Fruhauff	Megan Pooler	Alex Francis
		Whitney Martin
Contributing Editor	**Developmental Editor**	Grace Seeman
Amy Peterson	Alex Wesley Moore	Kendra Smalley
		Mary Helen Thompson
Fiction Editor	**Graphic Designer**	Leila Vanest
Aaron Housholder	Kaitlyn Gillenwater	Sarah Wehlage

Relief Logo
Emily Schmidt

Relief: A Journal of Art and Faith is published annually. The journal is dedicated to advancing writing that exhibits high literary standards and doesn't shy away from our difficult and beautiful reality. E-mail can be directed to Daniel Bowman Jr., dan@reliefjournal.com, or visit our website Contact page to reach other editors.

Subscriptions, single issues, back issues, and Relief merchandise can be purchased at **reliefjournal.com.**

Visit our website to donate, or for more information on current staff needs or contact dan@reliefjournal.com for other offers of talent.

Relief accepts poetry, fiction, creative nonfiction, and graphic narrative. Visit **reliefjournal.com** to review guidelines and submit work. Sorry, but we do not read or return submissions by mail.

Front and back cover art is by Brenton Good, Associate Professor and Chair of the Department of Art & Design at Messiah College. Visit **brentongood.com** for more.

TABLE OF CONTENTS

From the Editor's Desk   6

Editor's Choice Awards   8

Contributor Bios   10

Carly Gelsinger   Believing Will Never   15
                         Come Easy Again

Chris Anderson   Transfigurations   20

                         You Never Know   21

Hillary Jo Foreman   Victoria! Victoria.   22

Jeddie Sophronius   Conversation with a Bleeding   28
                         God in My Arms

                         Death of the Chinese in Me   29

Suzanne Rhee   Endurance   31

Jeremiah Webster   Letter to my Grandson   37
                         (Who is probably a Cyborg)

                         New Normal   38

                         Gospel   39

Susanna Childress   Age Appropriate   40

Jeff Newberry   Satin Flowers in Graveyards   56

                         Aubade on Black Rock Mountain   57

Meredith Stewart   What I Think It Will Be Like   58
Kirkwood   to Be Married to You

Laura Arciniega	The Shell	60
James Allman, Jr.	Salt	70
Sarah Davis	What She Must See	72
Rachel E. Hicks	It Wasn't Odd	76
	Just Before	77
Tania Runyan	You'll Know When It's Ready	78
	Sestina for Flu Season	80
D.L. Mayfield	The Irritable Woman: Some thoughts on mothering, pride, ambition, and despair	82
Prasanta Verma	Expand-istan	88
	Lighting	89
	Steward	91
Marjorie Stelmach	Salt	93
	Vinegar	95
Julie L. Moore	Silent Night	97
Jeannie Prinsen	Lakeside, with Jonathan	115
Kimberly Ann Priest	On Needing Someone to Be a Little Like God	116
	Consider the Loquat	117

Andrew Koenig	The River	119
Ben Egerton	/siːdz/	124
Lisa Muir	Waiting on Trillium	130
Laurel Eshelman	The First Mulberry	137
Courtney O'Banion Smith	The Viewing	138
Jim Richards	Pure Speculation	140
Christie Purifoy	A Review of Jessie Van Eerden's *The Long Weeping: Portrait Essays*	141

FROM THE EDITOR'S DESK

Daniel Bowman Jr.

Dear reader:

As always, I'm so thankful you found us.

To shepherd fine writing into the world remains the most critical mission of *Relief*. I see the volume and quality of the writing herein as a sign of our continued importance in the complicated, exciting art-and-faith space.

I often teach a short essay by Enuma Okoro called "Faith Imitates Art." Okoro speaks of art-making as ". . . a striving for more, a . . . hunger for transcendental realities that can only be shaped out of what has already been given to us, unlike God who creates out of nothing. But . . . such creative shaping can also lead to new realities we can live into." The writers in this issue show us the transcendental power of everyday moments, and in turn, their artful exploration of those moments nudges us toward something better.

We're pleased to give you a wealth of great poetry in the *Relief* tradition, including several sestinas by our dear friend Tania Runyan, some beautiful poems by Jeff Newberry, and new work by the talented young Jeddie Sephronius. Speaking of youth, the 2018 issue features multiple emerging fiction writers who light up the page, and perhaps give us glimpses of the future of serious faith-fueled short stories.

In his essay "Faith and Fiction," Ron Hansen says that we look to literature for ". . .self-understanding, for analogies of encounter, discovery, and decision that help us contemplate and change our lives." Deeply personal essays here by D.L. Mayfield and Carly Gelsinger offer just such analogies for the reader of open heart and mind, while longer CNF pieces from poets Susanna Childress and Julie L. Moore take on nothing short of death and loss, family, race, identity, community, and much more.

This is the second issue of *Relief* to be developed with the help of students in my ENG 470: Literary Editing and Publishing class at Taylor University. This year, our staff grew from four to ten. I can't overstate the impact of this group of talented young editors on the overall look and feel of *Relief* as the journal continues to evolve. Each voice added something significant to the 2018 issue through many hours of reading and discussion. Thank you, Samantha, Mary, Kaylen, Alex, Whitney, Grace, Kendra, Mary Helen, Leila, and Sarah. Thank you, too, to contributing editor Amy Peterson, developmental editor Alex Wesley Moore, and graphic designer Kaitlyn Gillenwater.

Readers: we hope *Relief* Spring 2018 challenges and edifies you. Have a great summer. Writers: submissions open up again in October, and we're eager to see your best work.

Until then,
Dan

Daniel Bowman Jr.
Editor-in-Chief, *Relief*
Upland, IN | May 2018

EDITOR'S CHOICE AWARDS

The Relief *Editor's Choice comments are not meant to indicate the "best" work in the issue, but instead to highlight something of abiding interest, some element that has captured our imagination. We see this as an opportunity to begin a discussion, one that is rooted in our mission, and that we hope will continue among readers.*

POETRY Three Poems by Jeremiah Webster

In the fall of 2017 I read Jeremiah Webster's collection After So Many Fires. *The pace, cadence, and syntax of his poems creates a unique, honest voice that I find to be deeply compelling. The poems, in the book and here in the pages of* Relief, *contain equal parts humor, prophetic lament, and a complicated kind of hope. Webster gives us an incarnate, open-eyed faith; one that rejects cynicism, but also rejects trite answers.*

—John Ballenger, Poetry Editor, *Relief*

FICTION "The Shell" by Laura Arciniega

It should come as no surprise that I love every piece of fiction in this issue. I love them all especially because they come from angles I've never seen before; they're driven by voices I've never heard in fiction. My mind keeps returning, though, to Laura Arciniega's "The Shell" for the singular irregularity of its tone and texture, and specifically for its playful consideration of the passage of time. And here's my favorite part: the narrative never explains itself. It moves forward, driven by whimsical narration and lovely language and lasting imagery, and asks you to keep up as you can and not worry about it. This story does for me what the best stories do: it grabs me early, sets its own rules, and proceeds on the trajectory it sets for itself, assuming I'll come along. The story expects me to do some work as I read and then makes that work most rewarding. Every story in this issue is a masterpiece, in my view, but "The Shell" haunts me for the enchanting control it exerts on the reader.

—Aaron Housholder, Fiction Editor, *Relief*

NONFICTION "The Irritable Woman: Some Thoughts on Mothering, Pride, Ambition, and Despair" by D.L. Mayfield

I adore each of the four brilliant essays in this issue. Yet it's D.L. Mayfield's "The Irritable Woman: Some Thoughts on Mothering, Pride, Ambition, and Despair" that hasn't let go of me these many weeks. In a world of ever-sensational clickbait and soundbites, it's a quiet, internal piece with a deep if subtle vulnerability at its core. The word "vulnerability" derives from the Latin noun vulnus: wound. *For a CNF writer to invite a reader toward immersion, reflection, and ultimately even a path of healing, she must possess both the willingness to examine her own wounds and the insight to articulate that interior terrain. Mayfield has both in spades, along with warmth and humor. And her particular brand of vulnerability here is so personal—so related to her intertwined identities as a writer, parent, spouse, and more—I dare say it's braver than it appears.*

—Daniel Bowman Jr., Editor in Chief, *Relief*

CONTRIBUTOR BIOS

James E. Allman, Jr.'s credentials—degrees in biology and business—qualify him for an altogether different trade. However, he easily tires of the dissected and austerely economized. He is a dabbler with an expensive photography-habit and a poetry-dependency. Nominated for three Pushcart Prizes, his work appears, or is forthcoming, in *Black Warrior Review, The Literary Review, Nimrod, Phoebe, Prairie Schooner, Sugar House Review,* and *Third Coast,* among others. He's written reviews for *Rattle* as well as other journals, blogs and sundries and is the co-founder of an artist community called Continuum. Follow him on Facebook @JamesEAllmanJr and Twitter @jallmanjr or visit his blog to read more of his work: jameseallmanjr.wordpress.com.

Chris Anderson is a professor of English at Oregon State University, a Catholic deacon, and author of a number of books, including poetry and prose.

Laura Arciniega holds an MDiv from Beeson Divinity School. Her work has appeared in *Burnt Pine Magazine, Mad Scientist Journal, Rascal Journal, Eastern Iowa Review* and *Saint Katherine Review*. Originally from Southern California, Laura and her husband Dominic Zappia now live in Bayonne, New Jersey with their son. You can find Laura online at lauraaliciaarciniega.wordpress.com and on Twitter @LauraAArciniega.

Susanna Childress has published two books of poetry. A book of essays, titled *Extremely Yours,* is forthcoming from Awst Press. She lives, teaches, parents, sings, flails, and glows in Holland, MI.

Sarah Davis recently graduated from Taylor University with a degree in journalism, quietly fueled by her love of creative writing. All of her stories are written as worship.

Ben Egerton is a poet and education lecturer from Wellington, New Zealand. He is currently studying for a creative PhD in poetry and theology at the International Institute of Modern Letters at Victoria University of Wellington, where his interests lie in the articulation of faith and experience through contemporary poetry. Ben's poems, and writing about education, are readable or forthcoming in such places, among others, as the *Times Educational Supplement* (UK), *The New Zealand Herald* (NZ), *Cordite Poetry Review* (Aus), *Turbine | Kapohau* (NZ), *Swamp* (Aus), *Eyewear Review* (UK) and *Landfall* (NZ).

Laurel Eshelman writes from rural Illinois where she works with her husband at Eshelman Pottery. Her chapbook, *The Red Mercy*, was a semifinalist in the 2014 Palettes and Quills Chapbook Contest and her poems have appeared in *Sixfold*, *The Phoenix Soul*, and *The Prairie Wind*.

Hillary Jo Foreman recently graduated from Taylor University with a degree in English/Creative Writing. In the fall, she will begin working toward her MA in Fiction at Ohio University.

Carly Gelsinger lives in California with her husband and two daughters. She holds a master's in journalism and runs a small business helping people write their stories. Her first book, *Once You Go In: A Memoir of Radical Faith*, releases in the fall of 2018.

Rachel E. Hicks' poetry has been published in *St. Katherine Review*, *Off the Coast*, *Gulf Stream Literary Magazine*, *Welter*, *The Penwood Review*, *Bloodstone Review*, and other literary journals. Her poem "Birth of the Girl-Child" won the second-place prize for the Maryland Writers Association 2016 Writing Contest. In addition, online magazines and blogs (e.g., *A Life Overseas*, *antler*, *Velvet Ashes*, *Thrive!*) have published several of her essays. You can see samples of her work on her website, rachelehicks.com.

Meredith Stewart Kirkwood's poetry has appeared or is forthcoming in *Eastern Iowa Review*, *Right Hand Pointing*, *Atlanta Review*, *Rock & Sling*, *Windfall*, *VoiceCatcher 6*, and others. In addition, one of her poems was selected to be republished in the anthology *She Holds the Face of the World: 10 Years of VoiceCatcher*. She lives in the Lents neighborhood of Portland, Oregon where she co-hosts a reading series at the farmers' market. Find her on the web at mkirkwoodblog.wordpress.com.

Andrew Koenig is a writer living in Chicago, IL. He received his MFA in Creative Writing from Seattle Pacific University and is the associate fiction editor for Saint Katherine Review.

D.L. Mayfield lives and writes in Portland, OR. Her essays have appeared in publications like *Image, Ruminate, Geez, The Rumpus,* and *Sojourners*. Her book *Assimilate or Go Home: Notes from a Failed Missionary on Rediscovering Faith* (HarperOne) was released in 2016.

A previous contributor to *Relief,* **Julie L. Moore** is the author of four collections of poetry, including *Full Worm Moon* and *Particular Scandals,* both published in The Poiema Poetry Series by Cascade books. Moore's poetry has also appeared in *Image, New Ohio Review, Poetry Daily, Prairie Schooner, The Southern Review,* and *Verse Daily*. An Associate Professor of English and the Writing Center Director at Taylor University, Moore worships at R.E.A.L. Community Covenant Church, a congregation dedicated to multi-ethnic community and racial reconciliation in Marion, Indiana. You can learn more about her work at julielmoore.com.

Lisa Muir is the author of the short-story collection *Taking Down the Moon*. She lives at the top of a mountain in Boone, NC, and teaches English at the bottom of the mountain at Wilkes Community College. Her work has also appeared in *Affinity: An Anthology, College Literature,* and *Centennial Review,* among others. She looks forward to seeing her novel, *Water Pressure,* published soon.

Jeff Newberry is a Professor of English at Abraham Baldwin Agricultural College in Tifton, Georgia, where he teaches in the Writing and Communications program. He serves as an advisory editor for *Pegasus,* the student-run literary journal. His most recent book is the novel *A Stairway to the Sea*. He has published a poetry collection and a chapbook. Recently, his writing has appeared in *The MacGuffin, Xavier Review,* and *Mary: A Journal of New Writing,* whose editors awarded his essay "Name" the Author's Prize for that issue.

Kimberly Ann Priest is the author of *White Goat Black Sheep* (FLP) and her poetry has appeared in several literary journals including *The 3288 Review, Temenos, Borderlands: The Texas Poetry Review,* The *West Texas Literary Review, Windhover, Ruminate Magazine,* and *The Berkeley Poetry Review*. A recent MFA graduate of New England College, she currently lives in Oklahoma where she is an English Instructor at Oklahoma Baptist University and an editor for the *Nimrod International Journal*.

Jeannie Prinsen lives with her husband, daughter, and son in Kingston, Ontario, where she teaches an online course in essay-writing at Queen's University. Her poetry has previously appeared at *Altarwork* and *The Bangor Literary Journal*. Jeannie's poems, short stories, and blog posts (at "Little house on the circle" – prinsenhouse.blogspot.ca) mostly explore her interest in faith, personal growth, family, memories, nature, and autism—and her poem "Lakeside, with Jonathan" touches on all these themes. As a parent of two autistic teens, she is increasingly aware of the importance of listening to autistic voices of all kinds.

Christie Purifoy is a writer and gardener who lives with her family in a Victorian farmhouse in southeastern Pennsylvania. She holds a PhD in English literature from the University of Chicago and is the author of two books, *Roots and Sky* (Revel, 2016) and *Placemaker* (Zondervan, coming in 2019).

Suzanne Rhee is a writer and comic artist from Fort Wayne, Indiana. She is an artist resident at Artlink Gallery's 212 Arts Incubator, and is beginning an MFA at Seattle Pacific University.

Jim Richards' poems have been nominated for *Best New Poets*, two Pushcart Prizes, and have appeared recently in *Sugar House Review, Prairie Schooner, Poetry Northwest, Southern Poetry Review, South Carolina Review, Juked, Comstock Review, Cumberland River Review* and others. He lives in eastern Idaho's Snake River valley and has received a fellowship from the Idaho Commission on the Arts. Find him at jim-richards.com.

Tania Runyan is the author of the poetry collections *What Will Soon Take Place, Second Sky, A Thousand Vessels, Simple Weight,* and *Delicious Air*, which was awarded Book of the Year by the Conference on Christianity and Literature in 2007. Her guides *How to Read a Poem, How to Write a Poem,* and *How to Write a College Application Essay* are used in classrooms across the country. Her poems have appeared in many publications, including *Poetry, Image, Harvard Divinity Bulletin, Christian Century, Saint Katherine Review,* and the Paraclete book *Light upon Light: A Literary Guide to Prayer for Advent, Christmas, and Epiphany*. She was awarded an NEA Literature Fellowship in 2011.

Courtney O'Banion Smith has been a teacher of literature and writing for more than ten years and a mother of boys for more than five. Her poems and book reviews have appeared in several print and online publications, including *Southwestern American Literature, Alba*, and a featured post on *Poetic Asides*.

Born in Jakarta, Indonesia, **Jeddie Sophronius** is a senior at Western Michigan University, majoring in English with an emphasis in creative writing. His work has appeared or is forthcoming in Bridge, Watershed Review, Juked, and The Ear. He currently lives in Kalamazoo.

Marjorie Stelmach has published five volumes of poems, most recently *Falter* (Cascade). Previous volumes include, *Bent upon Light* and *A History of Disappearance* (University of Tampa Press) and *Without Angels* (Mayapple). Her first book, *Night Drawings*, received the Marianne Moore Prize from Helicon Nine Editions, and a selection of her poems received the first Missouri Biennial Award. A group of her poems received the 2016 Chad Walsh Poetry Prize from *The Beloit Poetry Journal*. In addition to *Relief*, individual poems have appeared in *American Literary Review, Boulevard, Florida Review, Gettysburg Review, Hudson Review, Image, The Iowa Review, New Letters, Poetry Daily*, and *Tampa Review*, among others.

Prasanta Verma was born under an Asian sun, raised in the Appalachian foothills of the deep south, and now lives amidst snow piles in the upper Midwest. She has an MBA from the University of Wisconsin-Milwaukee, and an MPH from the University of Alabama-Birmingham. She is a writer and poet and currently coaches high school students in debate.

Jeremiah Webster teaches literature and writing at Northwest University in Kirkland, Washington. His poetry has appeared in numerous journals including *North American Review, Crab Creek Review, Beloit Poetry Journal, Floating Bridge Review, The Midwest Quarterly, REAL, Dappled Things, Rock and Sling*, and elsewhere. *After So Many Fires* (Anchor and Plume, 2017) is his first collection.

BELIEVING WILL NEVER COME EASY AGAIN

Carly Gelsinger

Kevin is at my parents' house when I get home from school. His normal uniform of a white Hanes shirt and khakis are black with char, and his arms show deep red gashes. All day he's been helping my dad clear brush left over from the fire. His eyes light up when I walk in the house. My dad is grateful—and desperate—for the help. It's been six months since the forest fire burned everything down, and there is still so much work to be done.

But I know why Kevin is here. There is something heartbreaking about the way he sits on the couch of this modular home that my parents had shipped to the property after the fire. His crooked glasses coated with dust, he is exhausted but summoning his last bits of energy to smile at me.

I'm weary too. I can hardly remember an existence where Kevin wasn't hovering in the foreground. I mumble a hello and go straight to my room to start my homework. I appreciate the help for my family, but this isn't Bible times. Jacob of the Old Testament worked in the fields to earn the favor of Rachel's father, but who cares? It isn't happening here.

I'm only eighteen, but I already feel like my life hasn't gone as planned. Instead of becoming the world changer they said I'd be, the victorious woman of faith I dreamed of being, I dropped out of college because of this ache in my chest that won't go away, this constant loneliness. The fire wasn't caused by my family's sin, my pastor made a point of telling me. But I feel like it wouldn't have happened if I had more faith.

In the dark hours of early mornings, I've whispered the word *depression*, but I won't say it out loud. I'm not depressed. Depression is for people who don't love Jesus.

Kevin knocks on my door. I shout, "Come in!" in a tone that really means *Go away.*

"Hi, er, I was wondering if you wanted to hang out this week," he says, standing stiffly in my doorway.

"Sure, Kevin. I'll see you at youth group. Maybe we can all go to Starbucks after."

I have to treat him this way because any kindness I show him fuels his obsession. I've known Kevin has liked me ever since he gave me that journal two years ago, looking at me all meaningfully one night after youth group. It wasn't until after I got the journal home that I noticed he'd written a note to me in the inside flap in his perfectly proportioned geometric caps. I'd tossed the journal under my bed and wished the gift had come from someone cute.

The other girls at youth group tease me about him, because they think Kevin is gross, but I don't think there is anything gross or funny about the situation. I think it's sad. He is older than me and a little strange, and I feel sorry for him. I mean, I am dying for a boyfriend, but even I will never consider dating Kevin. Despite how hard he tries, his looks and personality, which he cannot change, just do not appeal to me.

"Yeah, that will be fun, but I was hoping to hang out with just you for a little bit. I need to tell you something," he says.

"Okay. What's up?"

"No. I'm not ready to tell you now," he says.

"Then...how about Wednesday? I'll meet you in the church parking lot. Four o'clock," I say.

"Yeah," he says. He is still standing, frozen.

"So I'll see you then," I wave him out of the doorway. "Bye."

It's Wednesday. We are sitting in my Honda Accord, parked outside the baseball diamond at the Pine Canyon Park where we used to come pray for revival. He had offered to drive, but I want control of this outing. I have no plan in mind, other than knowing I don't want to get food or coffee with him. The less festive and date-like this encounter is, the better.

Kevin smells disgusting, like he's been dumpster diving. He is staring at his lap in the passenger seat of my car. My family is going to the movies in an hour, so I don't have long. I'm waiting for him to tell me he likes me, and then I will politely tell him I don't share his feelings, so I can get to the movies in time for the trailers. But Kevin isn't spitting it out.

"So you needed to tell me something?" I say, prompting him.

Long pause, again. I look over at him. He's gelled his hair, and he's wearing a polo shirt. Oh gosh, he dressed up for the occasion. I can hardly bear the thought of him squeezing gel into his comb as he got ready today, thinking of me. Then again, if he gussied up, he could have at least showered off the stink.

"Well, what is it?" I say.

I want to say, *Look Kevin, this is never going to happen,* but I don't. These are words he needs to form. He gives me a desperate smile, and my heart aches for him. I had thought I wanted him to squirm today, to make him pay for all the obnoxious ways he's followed me around for years, but now that he's here, squirming, I want to comfort him. I realize the reason I'm here sitting with Kevin right now is because I care about him, and that I always have.

He lets out a huge sigh and closes his eyes. The sigh brings a wave of putrid, rotting death into the car, and I roll down my window, trying not to let him see my disgust.

"Carly. The day I met you four years ago, I went home thinking, 'What a girl,'" he says. "But I knew I didn't deserve you. You are so beautiful and godly and free, and I...I am not. So I went to sleep feeling like I'd lost the love of my life."

I look out the window, the strain in his voice almost too much for me to handle.

"But then, that night, I had a dream. In it, you were covered with tattoos. From head to toe," he says.

"Okay," I say, feeling sick.

"The tattoos were a script in Hebrew, but in my dream, the Lord translated them for me. They said, 'Carly: Loving wife to Kevin.' They said, 'Carly: Loving mother of four.' They said, 'Carly: beloved by God,'" he says.

I was hoping for an I-like-you-will-you-go-out-with-me conversation in which I would reject him kindly, easily, and I could make my movie. But I guess if that were all he had to say, he would have said it years ago. This is something else entirely.

"The dream was so vivid I woke from it, sweaty, with an urgent sense to write everything down. God was so near me that night as I cried out to him. I said 'God, but she's too good for me,' and God said 'She is yours if you live your whole life for me,' and I wept," he says.

"Wow, that's...interesting," I say. I sound like an idiot.

"So from that day forward, I trusted God on his promise. I read my Bible every day and made him the center of my life. I felt if the promise was to come true, I had to believe that it would. I had to treat you like my future wife as an act of faith. There were times I knew it bugged you, that you wanted me to leave you alone, and it was hard for me to trust God in those times . . . especially when I saw how much you liked . . . Danny," he says, his voice choking on the name.

"Let's not talk about Danny now," I say.

"So this is me, acting on that faith, and believing God, even when it doesn't make sense," he says.

My stomach turns upside down and I brace myself what comes next.

"Carly, will you prayerfully consider being my wife?"

He says this without looking at me, without a ring, without a history that would make the question remotely sane. His eyes are closed and he is heaving fast breaths as he waits for my answer.

"No," I say, turning to face him. "I am sorry, but my answer is no."

"I knew it would be," Kevin says, and his tears start to fall into his lap. "I knew it would be. I fasted for three days for this, hoping for the promise to be fulfilled, but I always knew you'd say no."

Fasting. That's why he stinks so badly. His guts are crying out for food and he's denied them for three days. Because of a dream he had four years ago. Because of a word from God. The words of a thousand sermons come back to me.

Believe in the promises.

Dwell in the Secret Place of the Lord and he will whisper revelations to you.

Fast and pray for miracles.

God has an incredible destiny for you.

But hearing them in practice now, with Kevin's heart smashed on the dashboard in front of us, their craziness comes into sharp focus. This is insane.

"I'm sorry," I say again, but I'm not sure what I'm apologizing for. "Maybe God meant something else by that dream, do you think?"

"No. I know what God meant. He said we would be together, if— and only if—I lived for him. I fell short of that. I didn't live up to my end of the promise. And I'll have to live with it the rest of my life."

Believe in the promises. I can hear our favorite revivalist saying it, his raspy voice filling the words with urgency and purpose. *Or don't,* I want to shout back at the preacher. *Don't believe the promises.* All these years, Kevin's been praying and believing and showering me with gifts because he believes in a promise, when all along there was nothing he could do to make me love him.

"Kevin, don't blame yourself. You could be the godliest man in the world and I still wouldn't—" I stop, realizing just how hurtful the end of that sentence would be to him. "And we still wouldn't be compatible." I hand him an In-n-Out napkin for a tissue. He wipes his cheeks and blows his nose.

"Without this dream, I don't know what I can believe in anymore," he says.

I want to think he's being manipulative, but his words are too familiar. They take me back to the day one year ago when I drove seven hours to visit the boy I thought God had promised me. Stiff from the drive but giddy and in love, I ran to his tall figure outside his church's fountain as fast as I could.

Danny, I'm here, I cried.

He pulled away from my hug.

Carly, I'd like you to meet my girlfriend, he said.

Before those eight words, believing came easy. Now it's a fight every day, and now in one word—*No*—I have done the same for Kevin. Believing will never come easy again.

"I know what you mean," I say, and he opens his eyes and looks at me.

"This dream got me through so much. Even when I knew it would never come true, even when every logical thing I knew about you and me told me it would never work, I clung to it."

I can restore his faith right now with a few simple words. I can prove that God exists and that he is good and that the promise Kevin believed isn't a lie. I can do that right now, for Kevin.

Instead, I tell him we can still be friends, feeling like a stupid cliché. The words are genuine, but so empty and small, so not enough for what he needs right now. Knowing this, I don't try to fill the void with more empty words.

I start my car.

He doesn't speak on the short drive back to the church. I steer to avoid the potholes in the parking lot, and pull up next to his 1970s Thunderbird that he is always fixing with duct tape. He gets out and looks at me with lost eyes, and I know he is saying goodbye.

"Eat something," I tell him, but he doesn't answer. He walks to his car without turning back.

TRANSFIGURATIONS

Chris Anderson

for Bob

When we climbed the Mount of Transfiguration
we didn't know your heart was failing.
You could have had a heart attack right there, at the top,
where we celebrated mass on that kind of patio
with the corrugated roof and Jesus may or may not have been
bathed in light. You were white as chalk. Short of breath.
I thought you were just tired. I was tired.
Remember all the garbage in the town at the foot of the hill?
The ugly little houses, square, dirty white?

For a moment today as they were cracking you open
and spreading back the layers I believed everything was true.
The bread really was the Bread.
The wine really was the Wine.
I didn't want to talk about it anymore or try to explain it.
It just was.

Do you remember the other Mount of Transfiguration,
on the way to the Golan Heights?
It could have happened there, too, at the source of the waters
of the Jordan. No one really knows.
I loved how smooth the water was as it curved over a shallow ledge.
Several caves rose up behind us and there was a high, grassy ridge,
but the water is what stays with me now,
and the coolness of the water,
and how clear and clean and simple it seemed. That glittering sheet.

YOU NEVER KNOW

Chris Anderson

All those countless centuries
before I was born it wasn't so bad.

I didn't feel a thing.

Is this what it's like when we die?
Do we just cease to exist?

Or do the angels come to greet us,
skimming over the bright green fields,
calling out our names?

When I had breakfast at the Senior Living Center,
the women all around us in their flowery blouses
and the men in their motorized chairs
chatted and laughed at their little tables
like kids in a school cafeteria,
and the sun streaked through the windows,
and the oatmeal steamed in our bowls,
and even my hunched and befuddled father
was smiling for a moment, almost coherent.

I couldn't have been
more surprised: how happy I was.

VICTORIA! VICTORIA.

Hillary Jo Foreman

ACT 1

You've come to look at me too? Well, come in, but don't bother holding out your hand like I'm going to shake it. I don't like to be touched. I don't even intend to turn around. That's why the mirror is set up this way. I can see you the moment you pass through my dressing room door, but your image of me is obscured by this film of hairspray and sporadic mascara calligraphy.

I hope you don't mind my reflection.

Usually when fans come up after a show, they've just seen me as Nora or Eurydice or Kate, and they're dying to see if I am in real life as I appeared onstage—really that foolish? that forgetful? that mean? They want their playbills signed by the character. They want their photo taken with the girl in the costume. They've lost track of reality, as people will in the theatre.

That's why, back in the 1930s, Bertolt Brecht staged his productions in front of alienating placards. They seemed to scream, "THIS IS A SOCIAL CRITIQUE," so instead of being entertained, audiences remembered to think. Not to dream but to be.

I set up my dressing room in the same way. The spherical makeup bulbs shine on me like spotlights. The rest of the room is dim, cluttered by old clothes and dusty textbooks. It's a small room, nowhere to hide, all of it reflected backwards in a dirty mirror. It's not the main stage, but it's mine, my new stage, and I embrace it. What else am I to do? I sit here quietly on my stool and read, wait to hear my name called from below.

I used to play traditional roles in front of traditional audiences, but the same manager who assigned me this lonely upstairs dressing room has also assigned me an unusual role. You seem pretty unusual yourself, here alone in the middle of the performance, so I'll let you in on a secret. I'm actually performing right now. Funny, right? More like ironic. I've played half a dozen characters that are nothing like me, and now that my role matches my reality, no one can see it.

But you're here now; why don't you take a seat. There by the costume rack is fine. Let me find you a script so you can follow along. Here, behind my melting face palette. Right now we're on page six. The weary Stage Door Keeper tells the Officer that no one is allowed in the dressing rooms, so he begins to pace anxiously outside the door, and the Goddess interprets it as love. She's just arrived to earth to experience human life for herself. She doesn't know that as he paces and paces, as he clutches the bouquet of red roses tighter and tighter, he's only thinking of Victoria's false lashes, of her hair falling over her eyes, of her robe falling off her shoulder.

Officer (with vibrato): Victoria!

Please excuse me.

Victoria: Coming!

That's it. I don't have to rush downstairs now and appear on cue or remember pages of words I would never really say. It's nice in a way. The show's director, also the manager, also the man playing the Officer, decided Victoria should not make an appearance, that only her voice should be heard, so I sit on my stool in my robe and exclaim my line through the open door. At first, the cast was unsure of his decision— Would the voice make any sense if the audience couldn't see the speaker?—but we've been running fifteen weeks, two performances per weekend, and we don't seem to be losing popularity.

But I keep this photo stuck here in the border of my mirror as a reminder that things change. Can you see the delicate ponies, the elaborate architecture, the frosty oval mirrors? My mother bought me this carousel for Christmas when I was a little girl, the year I asked for my own pet. I didn't care what it looked like or what species it belonged to; I only desired a companion, a genuine relationship with someone who wouldn't obsess about my canopy bed or my rainbow of a closet or anything else my mother's money brought home. Unfortunately, my mother didn't care much for things with the potential to stink or shed or die. She was practical; she purchased this carousel and had it installed in our backyard. Can you imagine? The sparkly lights and fairytale music— they were always at my disposal. Rather than one pony, I had ten to choose from, acrylic and beautiful.

You might think I was just a spoiled brat, but think of it this way: I wanted something to confide in, to cuddle while I cried. Have you ever sought empathy in hand-painted eyes or embraced a hollow statue? I was disappointed by the gift, but my mother expected my worship, so I pretended to love it, to find comfort and joy and all sorts of Christmastime emotions in the carousel. I dressed up in satin and rode sidesaddle. I fashioned myself like Equestrian Barbie and walked in circles for hours, leading my trained stallions around their enclosure. I brought them apples and carrots and brushed the air above their manes and tails so not to scratch their coating.

This photo gives me hope because, dazzling as they were, the carousel horses quickly grew tiresome to my child self, even to my childhood friends. Surely, in the same way, our audiences will tire of this production. Only fools are endlessly entertained by the rising, the falling, the turning round and round of false horses. The same can be said, I'm sure, of disembodied voices. I can only hope the same can also be said of bodies without voices.

INTERMISSION

This is the part of the show where the actor who plays the Stage Door Keeper goes backstage to get ready for the next act, and the Officer sneaks up the narrow, wooden stairs to my dressing room. Can you hear his footsteps?

No, no, you don't have to leave. Keep your seat. You can move those books if they're in your way. I'm just going to touch up my makeup.

I wonder what he'll think of you.

Hear that? The third stair from the top always makes a sound like an explosion, a pop that lets me know the show is about to begin. Two. One.

The Officer breezes through the open door. Before he makes it to me, he sees you in the corner of the mirror, pauses, whirls around. I think he's going to get angry, to ask you to leave. He eyes you up and down, and you blush, and he winks. He turns back toward me.

Officer: My little bird is happy to see me?

My chest deflates. I should have known nothing would change.

I was twenty-seven the first time he and I played complementary roles, the first time he stumbled upon my dressing room, the first time he entered like it was his own. I'm not twenty-seven anymore.

He tosses a flustered bouquet of roses on the dressing table and takes off his jacket. I rub one of the satiny, blood-colored petals between my fingers and try not to look in the mirror as he rolls his hands from wrist to fingertip around my shoulders and massages them.

Officer: Loosen up. You know it's better when you relax.

I glance up to the mirror. He grins at me from beneath the slight rim of his old-fashioned police hat. One of his hands slides south from my shoulder, eases beneath the edge of my robe. His other hand removes his hat, places it beside the bouquet. The plastic gold badge winks in the light as if to tease me. Its wearer neither serves nor protects, yet his authority stands.

I hold my breath.

The Officer stands me up like a prop, leans me forward onto my elbows on the dressing table. My robe falls open. It is cold. The sound of the zipper on his dress pants opening is cold.

It's okay; you don't have to look away. You can't see anything, not really, but you can close your eyes if it makes you feel better. Just listen to the table rattle as the Officer jolts me forward and back like a mechanical horse.

Isn't it funny that right now, while you are here, there are people like you downstairs? They stand and stretch and comment on the quality of the show thus far. They go to the restroom, buy overpriced candy bars and swallow them practically without tasting because there's no food allowed in the theatre. They power on their cell phones for three minutes to make sure they haven't missed anything important. They squint through the dim house lighting to read a director's note about dreams, about the imaginary, and when the lights flash to signal the resumption of the show, they have no better understanding of what they're seeing than before.

Do you?

Officer (gasping): Victoria.

He jerks me against the dressing table and the mirror wobbles to and fro, not really steady as it seems.

Officer: Say your line, sweetheart.

He used to shake me until I said it. Now he fixes his clothes, wipes the sweat from his forehead.

He snatches the bouquet, wilted under the heat of my makeup lights.

Exit.

ACT 2

There are six or seven more pages before my next line, my last line actually, so I hope you don't mind if I read for a while. I've been stuck for the last month or two on this book of sermons by John Wesley. I read the one about free will again and again, try to make myself believe like Wesley in decision, not destiny.

I think my father believed that way. He exercised his free will before I was born, abandoned his pregnant girlfriend, abandoned the child who, apparently, looks just like him. My mother could hardly bear to look at me because of it, so she purchased cases of makeup and colored my hair, but it wasn't enough, so she sold me to the entertainment industry. That's her in the photo beside the carousel. If only I'd looked so angelic as her, not so dark, not so angular. Maybe then I would have been worthy of her affection.

I'd like to ask Wesley where my free will was in all of that.

Or in this: the Officer's hat lingers on my dressing table like a bad excuse. He'll come back for it after tonight's show or before tomorrow's. I never know when he'll be here, when I might be expected to perform.

It didn't always feel like this, though I suppose I never consented. The first time was shortly after we started working together. I was twenty-seven and he was tireless. Back then he'd kiss me rough, scratch my soft neck with the stubble he probably ought to have been shaving for a role. Then this play *A Dream Play* rolled around, and he was so enthused by his success that he visited me every night, sometimes more than once, and shouted both our lines, exclamation points and all. But after we'd been running this same show in this same style for 71 nights, the script's exchange of exclamation marks for periods became audible in real life as well as on the stage. He used to linger past the climax to ask me about my family, my books, my thoughts. Back then I knew he wanted me; I thought I knew. Now he does what he must to get himself off and leaves without the slightest effort to share his pleasure. I've lost significance. Next I'll lose my job. Perhaps I'll lose my mind.

Meanwhile, the Goddess is whining downstairs. She's figured out that life is not as shiny as it seems. Her expectations are unfulfilled. Perhaps she thought her own carousel would make her special, but it turns out she's only small, only unimpressive beside it, so now she flies back to Heaven. She says, "Thanks, but no thanks. Human life is not for me."

Free will sounds nice, even realistic, maybe, to someone with such wings, but it's not so simple for an orphan, an actress, a slave.

I clap the crumbling, clothbound tome shut and drop it off the edge of my dressing table. I'm tired of free will, but—it's destiny—a maroon cover waits where Wesley once rested. All this time it must have been buried beneath. I scoot my hairbrush out of the way and peel the new book open to a middle section.

Psychology. Cartesian Dualism. Mind is distinct from matter.

If the mind and body are irreconcilable, what does that mean for the main and private stages, the actress and the woman, the lover and the victim? If these are separate entities, then I am even more fragmented than I used to think.

Officer: Victoria.

I meet your eye in the mirror, turn the page.

Victoria: Coming.

CONVERSATION WITH A BLEEDING GOD IN MY ARMS

Jeddie Sophronius

I wear red & white
The flag of my country
I am not white
I want to go home early
I can't move from where I am
With a bleeding God in my arms
I look around
I don't see anyone
I'm not a doctor
Just say grace
Father,
Thank you for this gathering—
I don't think that's how this works
Stay with me until I die
How long do stars take to explode?
You smell like chamomile & porridge
Can you take me with you?
Do you believe in me?
I don't know
Will I see you again?
I have questions about the Bible
I highlighted the contradictions
I didn't write everything in it
My mother is calling
She won't like it seeing me
Talking to a bleeding stranger
Tell her I'm a God
I don't know who to forgive
My sister or my childhood bully
Forgive both
I should go
I need to feed my dog
She's waiting for me two oceans away

DEATH OF THE CHINESE IN ME

Jeddie Sophronius

—*Jakarta, Indonesia.*

The Chinese boy in me was killed
when the authorities forced my mother to change her name

while her youngest sister sat under a pear tree
until little girls with almond eyes

could appear on the streets for anything other
than buying a pack of cigarettes or a bag of herbal tea.

& when I think of my father,
who doesn't speak with the tongue of a dragon,

I see how fortunate he is:
the people ignored the Chinese man in him.

My friend asked me once,
"Why do your people say *I* differently than mine?

We must use the same words,"
he said.

I couldn't answer him then, but I know:
our mothers are waiting under their umbrellas
for their sons to come back,

our sisters are hiding in the bathroom,
looking outside the window,
but their tears can't wash away the street names;

being *exotic* costs us our schools,
our stores, & our grandfathers burned or hanged on a pole.

Was it not enough when we stripped ourselves of our traditions

& cut the braids from our heads?

Under the burning sky lanterns,
a grandfather's hands are folded like a tulip on his chest,

his lips, chanting something in Chinese.
Beside him, a girl in a red dress asked,
"*Yéyé*, why do their guns
look like cranes?"

ENDURANCE

SUZANNE RHEE

A DIARY COMIC ABOUT GRIEF AND MOVING FORWARD

FEBRUARY

S	M	T	W	TH	F	S
				1	2	3
4	5	6	7	8	9	10
11	12	13	14	15	16	17
18	19	20	21	22	23	24
25	26	27	28			

THIS HAS BEEN A WEEK OF TEARS FOR ME...

I'm sorry, just give me a minute...

MY GRANDMOTHER DIED LAST SUNDAY. WE HELD HER FUNERAL ON SATURDAY.

Trying so hard to BREATHE

BUT WITH EVERY FAMILY GATHERING COMES FAMILY **DYSFUNCTION.**

ONE OF MY COUSINS TOOK THE LOSS ESPECIALLY HARD.

I WANTED TO HUG HER. BUT BECAUSE OF TENSIONS I DON'T UNDERSTAND, IT WOULDN'T BE RECEIVED.

INSTEAD, I HAD TO STAND AT A DISTANCE, LIKE I WAS **IGNORING HER.**

PRETENDING NOT TO LOVE MY OWN FAMILY? THAT HURT.

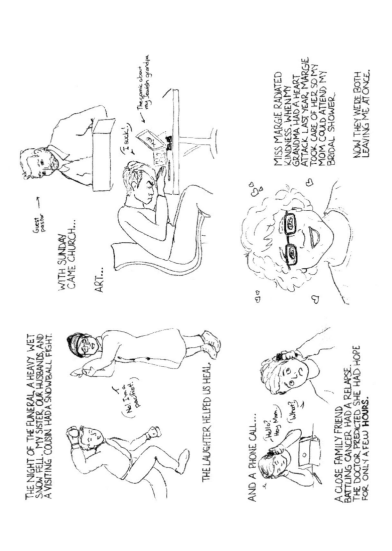

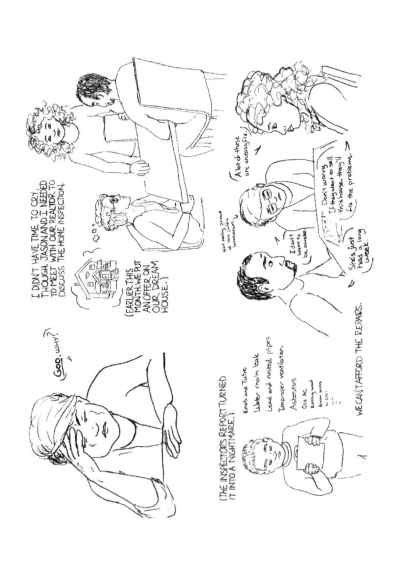

DESPITE GRIEF AND BAD NEWS, I KEPT MOVING FORWARD. THE COMICS PROJECT ABOUT MY GRANDPA BEGAN THE DAY AFTER GRANDMA GRACE, MY LAST SURVIVING GRANDPARENT, LEFT US: A SEAMLESS TRANSITION FROM LIVING WITH THEM TO REMEMBERING THEIR LIVES.

MISSING HER PROPELLED ME INTO MY WORK, WITH A STRANGE, ALMOST MANIC, INSISTENCE.

Grandpa Larry Rhee, German-Jewish emigrant, WWII U.S. Interrogator, Nuremberg Trials participant

I NEEDED THE ENERGY TO COMBAT THE PORTFOLIO REVIEW THAT I HAD THE FRIDAY BEFORE THE FUNERAL. MY REVIEWER, A SEASONED COMICS EDITOR, WAS KIND:

I'm new to comics. (This is all I have.)

Are you new to art? Your work displays unfamiliarity with the basic principles.

BUT ALSO HONEST:

Shoddy lettering... stiff paneling... inaccurate anatomy... no distinct style.... In fact, your work has decreased in quality over time.

You probably shouldn't attempt this large project until you have more practice.

oooh... that's icy. Don't cry.

...Yes, sir. Thank you, for your time.

GOD? | ARE YOU | LISTENING? | I can't do this.
Help me! | I SUCK.

Will anyone read this?

If you want me to do this than you have to show me how.

(I AM TOO ASHAMED TO TELL ANYONE. INSTEAD, I WRESTLE WITH SELF-DOUBT ALONE IN THE DARK STUDIO. I ALSO PRAY—HARD. GOD'S THE ONE WHO GOT ME INTO THIS.)

I BLAME, WHINE, AND BARGAIN.

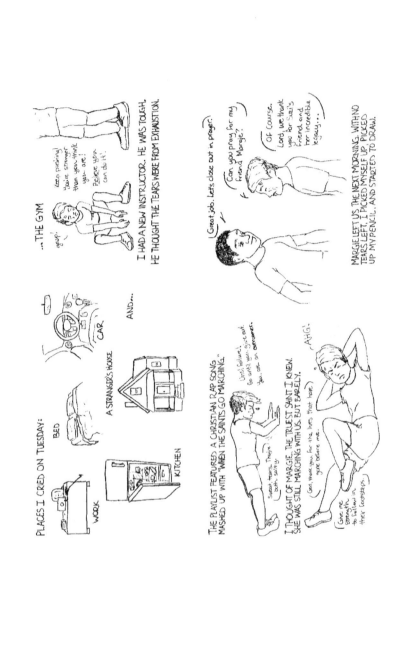

LETTER TO MY GRANDSON (WHO IS PROBABLY A CYBORG)

Jeremiah Webster

They tell me you have no use for the eyes nature gave you,
or the feet I called "miracle" on your birthday.
They tell me all identity is algorithm,
that you got a once-terminal cancer and lived, twice,
and that your mind has no use for the technology
of books I saved for you on shelves.
They tell me death eludes you, or you it,
and that you refused a trip to the Space Needle
after a tour in virtual reality.
They tell me the Internet is your beloved now,
that you said Mt. Rainier was "unreal"
the day it erupted for good.

I pray you know
grace abides,
meaning *the Lord*,
meaning *no upgrade necessary*,
in some region
of the synthetic organ
that is your heart.

NEW NORMAL

Jeremiah Webster

Redundant terrorism
arrives with the coffee.
Today, a bucket bomb,
detonated on the Tube.
Many injured.
No deaths.
This is called: progress.
Tomorrow, a rented van
will plough bodies more effectively
in one of Europe's dying promenades.

Blame religion.
U.S. foreign policy.
Middle East entire.
Psychos cut loose from a Hitchcock picture.
The banality of an "O, so Modern" world.
I say more. Age entire
slouches toward extinction.
Parents push bewildered strollers.
Children recite liturgies of the dead.
Crow skull becomes a talisman.
Ringtone, sufficient dirge.

And what innocence
when my son declares,
"There is no silence here

for God," not knowing chaos
awaits.

GOSPEL

Jeremiah Webster

Do stories fail,
negate themselves,
seek haven with huckster,
heathen, hang their promise from the rafters
like David Foster Wallace: the progress
of enlightened centuries?

Is the world content with a world
where the bones of nymphs, gnomes
preserved in enviable revelry, are never found,
where leviathan has no dominion,
where flowers are only caught, crushed in the machinery,
where Leda receives no recompense,
where Frodo is left for dead?

Here I am, near forty in good health,
educated beyond what is healthy for a man,
deferential (though discontent) in the ossified Cartesian mold,
seeking word beyond death,
word without end . . .

procreative torso,
starfish limb,
dormant seed,
empty tomb.

AGE APPROPRIATE

Susanna Childress

My son knows I had a baby in my tummy and then, after a surprise trip to the hospital during a blizzard, I didn't. He knows the baby died. He calls this baby by the name we have chosen, Jericho. He knows it happened again, a second time, though *that* baby was no bigger than a strawberry. That baby didn't get a little yellow hat of yarn or held in our arms or pictures taken. That baby wasn't a boy or a girl, only a strawberry who slipped away in the summertime, so we named it Tiernan, which is a boy's and a girl's name at the same time.

***

My son stands in my closet, stripped down to nothing, piling up oversized pillows to reach for my clothes. He pulls the orange sleeve of a blouse until it pops off the hanger, then a billowing dress of brown silk. He discards them both on the floor.

Son, I say, what's happening here?

Mama, he asks, Do you have anything for a Fairy Queen?

He is four, his naked body all vine and melon, a shimmering of knees, lobes, belly, knuckles, things he doesn't yet know how to dream. He's never heard of Spenser, and I have no idea where he's come by this phrase, or what he imagines a fairy queen might wear. I gamely paw through the options anyway, remembering the epic poem I'd studied with zero enthusiasm in grad school. How was it spelled, something like, F-a-e-r-i-e?

When I turn around, my son has found the plastic hospital bag I buried in the back of the closet, and, in a foggy, slow-motion sort of stupor, I watch him pull out the small purple sateen box that holds his dead brother's footprints, certificate of death, the only photographs we have of him. He shakes the box, and it offers the secretive *huck-huck* of its contents shifting back and forth. He touches the purple ribbon holding tight the box's top. I can see he wants to untie it, his fingers twitching toward the ends of the bow, but something stops him. He looks at me.

What is this, he asks, and then, when I fail to answer, asks again. What is this?

Outside my sister's home in Adete, Togo, on the cement portico where they leave Nolan's bats and balls, the ground is littered with thin green petals. No, my sister says. Termite wings. They've taken to the foundation.

In West Africa, as in much of the world, termites feast on human structures. What is proportion, what is purveyance: the cost of inhabiting this shared earth?

My son loves looking at my sister's Facebook page; it's full of photographs and videos of his cousin and the home where they live and the hikes they take, half a world away. We look up 'termites in West Africa.' We look up 'termite mounds.' We look up 'termite damage.'

I like bugs, my son says. Just not the kinds that sting things or bite things or eat things or crawl all over things. He pauses. That's maybe *all* of them?

Then he leaps from my lap: Let's read!

And so we do—the kids' book of West African bugs my sister sent for Christmas, each small square page glossy with a high-detail photograph of an insect and a pithy little sentence.

Some bugs are fancy. Some bugs are feathery. Some bugs are plain.

***

The year we lose Jericho so many things seem to shatter all at once, not just my body's betrayal to two babies, or theirs to mine, but also my husband's work and emotional health, my father's kidneys during a trip to Togo, the outbreak of Ebola in West Africa, the deaths of Michael Brown, Eric Garner, Tamir Rice, among others—by the end I truly don't know what's appropriate to tell my four-year-old and what to save from him.

Or is it *save him from?*

That troubling line in parenting: you want to save but you can't—at the very least, you're responsible for keeping them alive and at the very most, thriving on all levels. It's tempting to let yourself be confused about this at every turn.

One day, standing between the class turtles and the coat room, I broach the subject of death with my son's preschool teacher, a woman whose kind eyes and taste in sensible shoes make her seem unflappable:

how might I help my son understand? I am, of course, thinking of Jericho (we'd not yet lost Tiernan) but untimely, senseless, at-large (if not untimely, senseless, up-close) death feels unsuitable for my conversations with my son, as though I'm trying to fit these huge, unwieldy objects—a life-size ceramic rhino, say—in quaint, ridiculously dainty packages—like a handful of jewelry boxes.

His teacher blinks at me from behind her glasses. She hugs me. She sends me home with several photocopied sheets with tips on what to cover and what to avoid. Instead of "Grandpa is sleeping" or "Don't cry. You'll see Grandpa again one day," we should aim to be as literal and straight-forward as possible: "Grandpa's body stopped working, which is what caused him to die," and "Grandpa's not coming back," and "It's okay to cry. We all miss him." Lots of assurance and follow-up and safe touch and good sleep and freedom to question. The packet has a short paragraph on cultural customs surrounding funerals. Another paragraph on the loss of pets.

I'm grateful. I read each page several times over. And yet: grandpas and goldfish aren't exactly going to help me with a baby brother who died in utero. Or Ebola. Or black men shot in the back by law enforcement. As much as I appreciate the straightforwardness of these pages, the advice feels a bit too breezy.

Or maybe I'm asking too much. Maybe it's not really *death* I need help with but *grief*.

I type 'what to tell a child' into a search engine, and then add 'police brutality,' 'joblessness,' 'stillborn,' 'depression,' 'communicable disease.' Most sites have a helpful suggestion or two, chief among them *age-appropriate words, ideas, and images*.

Of course, one might think. Certainly. Duh, one might be inclined to say.

In general, I agree with the use of age-appropriate language and visuals; I'm all for not demonstrably terrifying the children. Let's please, for the love, help them feel safe and attended to and able to trust our (restrained, highly edited, carefully worded) forthrightness. But what 'age appropriate' means, how it's interpreted, the intrinsic seepage of parenting style and political ideals and religious beliefs, make all the murkier how and what and when I choose to say what I need to say to my son, a white boy from a Christian family in a small, Midwestern, North American town.

***

Before Ebola, my sister and her husband's chief concern was cancer—the country has not a single oncologist. Another chief concern: premature labor. And electrocution. And accidental strangling. And third-degree burns. And twins, all manner of twins, which in West Africa is as typical as singletons are elsewhere.

In Adete, Togo, as in much of the world, the travel and costs are prohibitive such that patients only come to the hospital—its catchment area is half a million people—with the most dire, the most deadly of ailments. My sister and her husband have had to reckon with the implacable: they are not saviors. They work shift on top of shift on top of shift; many, many of their patients will not survive.

No children's book exists for this, of course. No high-detailed glossy photos of the ones who, if they lived where my son and I live, might've survived. But even this is not altogether true. Black women in the U.S., for instance, have markedly higher maternal morbidity—the most recent research indicates as much as five times higher—than Caucasian women.

And we've not yet begun to consider Ebola, which never did reach Togo but was contained in Sierra Leone, Guinea, and Liberia, killing 11,315 people.

Which is to say, we don't have to consider Ebola. Not really. We can find age-appropriate words, ideas, and images for my son to let him know he is safe, safer, safest. No Ebola here, buddy, nobody you know with Ebola. But where are the age-appropriate words to examine why the only time anyone in the U.S. talks about an epidemic is when it is a threat to us? One fellow in Dallas endangered us all. Because Black people = dangerous. One white American doctor became a hero. Because white Americans = imminently good/saviors. Otherwise, you know, so what: it's just eleven thousand dead West Africans.

The shocking number of Black women who die during or after childbirth here in the states: is there a similar referendum of silence surrounding this, too?

Some people are fancy. Some people are feathery. Some people are plain.

***

My son finds me face down on the floor. I am trying to stifle my weeping in the gray weave of the carpet. My hands are slicked with mucus, my lungs hitching at the back end of each sob. I hear him behind me, my name in his mouth not a question but the soft-lilt of a song.

He's seen me like this before, laid low with sorrow. He doesn't know it, but this time it's not about a baby. It's not a Togolese patient. This time it's a white man walking into an AME church and, after sitting with worshippers through a Bible study and listening to their prayers, pulling out a gun and shooting them. Again and again he shot. Because they were Black. Because they are Black people. He shot them, in the basement of their church, as a racist, to incite a race war—

What's a race war, Mama? What's a racist?

These, somehow, are questions I can answer. But the project of being a parent is also the project of being a human: it's the ones that follow—the *but whys*—that I cannot, history's spiraling back into hate and greed and power, the warping and leaping to end up right back in the present. He's just turned five, has picked out a raccoon lunchbox to take to kindergarten in the fall and practices his colors in Spanish when we go for walks in the unfurling of June—already he can trill *amarillo*'s 'r', though the same sound in *negro*, in reference to a car, makes me flinch.

Because white people are broken. Or, evil. Which one is more age appropriate?

***

On an unseasonably warm day in January—the high hit nearly 60 degrees—my son's friend, Adam, invites him to Captain Sundae's after school. My son ejects himself from his booster seat, throws his wrists in the air like Kermit the Frog.

Yeah! he shouts. Yeah! Please?

Adam's mother rarely sugars up my son. We're on the same page about these things; we, like our children, are friends. Our sons are five together. They wipe their noses on their sleeves, have trouble sharing their scissors, try trading their grapes for peanut butter cups. They stack My-Dad-Can stories against each other like a tower of monster trucks. Our sons are in the same sunny public school classroom in the two-way bilingual immersion program. They're not yet fluent in Spanish, but they know the word *helado*. They have elaborate *helado* visions, dreams, plans:

sprinkles and globs of warm chocolate sauce and buttered pecans and cherries and caramel and whipped cream.

All roads, for the five-year-old, lead to Captain Sundae's.

That balmy winter day, my son comes home sticky and full of glee. His sundae had hot chocolate powder mixed in it. Yes, he had a great time. Yes, he said thank you for taking me.

Then I get a text from Phoebe, Adam's mom. Apparently, a hiccup.

The boys had asked to play outside on the "Captain's ship"—a large, wooden boat structure—after they'd finished their ice cream. Phoebe agreed, as long as they stayed where she could see them while she got Adam's little sister ready to go. But the boys hid. And when Phoebe called for them, they didn't answer. She called and they wouldn't come.

So, Phoebe writes, I may have gotten a little intense.

My son claimed he didn't understand the rule to go only where he can be seen because it's not one his mom has. (Not true.) Adam conveyed that my son prompted him to do it. (I believe this.) Phoebe reminded Adam that it doesn't matter what his friends tell him to do because he follows Mom's rules first.

Then, she texts me, I reminded Adam of our rule: if you are playing and a cop walks up, even if your friends run, YOU CANNOT RUN.

She writes: I wanted to give you a heads up in case he says, 'Uh . . . Phoebe was talking about the police,' and you think, 'Huh . . . that's pretty heavy for a quick, after-school outing.'

My son had said nothing to his father or me. Perhaps he was nonplussed because we talk about this—the ways people of color are treated differently than whites and what a white person's responsibility is when she sees or suspects that enacted. That white people have to be on the lookout for it even if it doesn't personally affect them. That, often, white people benefit from it. Which means, even more so, white people need to speak up, to act.

I've not been able to have this conversation without getting choked up, less weepy than sober and wet-eyed. My son has sensed, despite my fumbling, this is serious, tough stuff.

And yet, how would Phoebe know that? How could she assume my son's been exposed to the ideas of white privilege, racial bias, police brutality?

Parents with children of color don't have a choice about these conversations the way I do; they don't get to wonder *if* they should broach the topic, and how tenderly. Nothing about 'the talk,' as far as I've gathered, can afford to be tender, except maybe what that roiling desire to keep your child safe does to your innards.

Phoebe texts: I just get super intense about interactions with Adam and the public because I'm so nervous about him being profiled and targeted. Him hiding where people in the drive-thru can see him but I can't—things like that freak me out. I don't have those expectations for your son, so I wasn't giving him a hard time about it. But I can see him sometimes being a little confused about why I'm way more intense about particular things.

What occurs to me while I'm texting Phoebe is that, though we talk about it, what happened at Captain Sundae's may be the first time it's more than an idea to my son, the first time, if ex post facto, that it's a reality. Perhaps my work following up with him in the weeks, months, years to come is to make clear that attending to the reality with intention and not solely emotion is very, very important. He can't just feel sad or mad about his friend being perceived and treated differently than he is; instead, he needs to question: how does my own behavior affect the circumstances, how could my own actions and/or attitude make things better or worse for Adam, even if it doesn't make things better or worse for me?

The unfairness of it pricks the back of my tongue, that my son's behavior will not weigh against my son the same way Adam's will against Adam, that Adam, like black children everywhere, must work harder, act better, excel more excellently to be perceived as on par with my son. But things have never been *fair*. What whole systems—of which I'm implicitly a part—remain to be dismantled before they will be?

My phone buzzes with a text from Phoebe.

So, she writes, if as he gets older, he ever brings it up with you, you have a heads up as to why something like an innocent game of hide and seek makes Adam's mama start to talk about the police.

Earlier, she'd said this: I hope it wasn't too weird or over-intense for him.

I'm grateful for her thoughtfulness, that she felt compelled to make me aware but not apologize. Even so, my throat aches with questions I already sense the answer to. What if my son is not supposed to feel comfortable about this? What if I'm not supposed to either? What if our discomfort—the weirdness and over-intensity—is a natural, integral part of contending with how unfathomably weird and over-intense it is in this country for people of color all the time? What if our discomfort is part of displacing white experience as the most central, the most valid, the most valuable? What if our discomfort is part of slowly unbuckling the skewed systems, one kid, one mama at a time?

Which is to say, what work could discomfort do, if we let it? Am I willing to be uncomfortable? Is my son?

***

Some days the updates my sister sends, of her most recent patient, of an emergency case, rattle me like a bad dream. I cannot shake them. Almost all are likely death sentences: a woman with cancer of the throat; a woman with cervical cancer; a child with meningitis; a man with Lassa fever; a premature baby at 28 weeks—the mother's longest gestation after two other fatal preterm births. No, I cannot shake the shadow of the gulf: 28 weeks in the U.S. has a 90% survival rate; 28 weeks in Togo means this woman needs to start planning a funeral. Again.

I can't help this, either: I pray for the mothers and babies the hardest. Culturally, being a mother means something different in Togo— a woman's entire worth in her family and in the community is dependent on having children. But being a human is no different in Togo: losing a child is the language no one should have to speak, but those of us who have had to, we understand each other perfectly.

Sometimes my sister sends me pictures of the preemies under their blue heat lamps. Unlike photos of preemies here in the U.S., the babies aren't hooked by a dozen cords to machines. But their mottled, translucent skin, their impossibly tiny hands and feet, their limp, bony arms and legs: it's so familiar. I pray and I cry and I pray. Sometimes, usually when he asks me what's wrong, I show the pictures to my son.

These are the triplets Aunt Lillian delivered, I say. They're having a very hard time staying alive. So, she asked me to pray.

Am I being too heavy, too world-weary? Am I using age-appropriate words and ideas? Is this an age-appropriate image? Or is it more wrong *not* to show my son, *not* to mention it, to pretend that (especially) women and babies in Togo have the same chances of survival that they do here—*if* they're the right ethnicity, the right skin color? That, the world over, black bodies are—and here all the metaphors feel wrong, of war or currency—black bodies are under siege? Are worth less?

Sometimes, in a burst of hope and playfulness, we give the babies in these pictures Togolese names—Yawovi, Innocente, Koffi—and make up stories about them, how they'll live and grow. We comfort ourselves with this; we prioritize our comfort. We long for them to live. Yes, they will live and grow. Nolan will make friends with them, and they'll eat papaya together and play ball. They'll hike out to termite mounds. They'll take photos and post them, which we'll find online when we search.

Wow, we'll say, look at Yawovi! Can you believe the last picture we saw of him, he was only a pound and four ounces?

***

In the purple sateen box, Jericho's death certificate lists his weight: 9 ounces.

Sometimes his brother asks, Where is he?

Whether he's asking about an afterlife or the literal place where Jericho's body is, I'm uncertain. Well—well—well, I stammer, every time. Both are questions I should try to answer. But, without shame or presumption, I redirect: let's go get a snack, let's go read, let's find your leopard costume and play Wild Animals!

Perhaps I'd be able to frame the answers with age-appropriate words, ideas, and images, but I'm not ready to try.

I'm mad at heaven.

As for Jericho's body, how am I to explain that, under great emotional strain, hurried, we made a decision I regret entirely? Our options: bury, cremate, or allow the hospital to 'take care of the remains.' The expense and logistics of a burial—in a January blizzard—were beyond us; we could not imagine holding a funeral or memorial in part because of the complexities of the circumstance: I'd largely kept the pregnancy a secret, hiding my growing belly at my (part-time, adjunct) work because I was an internal candidate for a (full-time, tenure-track) nationally competitive position against three men; my husband was without work; my multi-day interview would be within the month. If I didn't get this job, we'd have no income and no prospects for another year. How could we hold a funeral? Or bury him in secret? It seemed too costly on every level.

We considered cremation but were told the ashes would be mostly blanket and wooden box. There would only be a teaspoon or so of *him*. And, again, the cost. Somehow, in that moment, having already been robbed of our baby's life, $900 felt like an insult, like too much for a teaspoon.

So, we chose the third option: the hospital would 'take care of the remains,' which means his tiny body—his 9 ounces—were incinerated, likely with the rest of the hospital's 'waste,' a heap of ashes swept away for the next round of rubbish.

Writing this out, it's hard not to hate myself for our decision. Are we such misers, such cowards? My son, my Jericho: gone. And I have not a thing in this world left of him—not a headstone, not a teaspoon. Nothing.

Of course, if I could speak of heaven, I'd point beyond this world. But I've not been able to find some immutable comfort in that possibility—about which my faith tradition has much lore, much cherubic, palatial to-do, but precious little scriptural evidence. I do believe in heaven. For all I know, my son might too. I'll talk to him at some point about heaven. But the questions that will follow—the *wheres* and the *hows* and the *what doeses*—I have nothing age-appropriate for that either. Maybe nothing at all.

Which means what I'm not yet ready to do, for his sake but likely for my own, is tell my son the truth. Where is your brother?

I don't know.

***

Nicole calls me on a Wednesday morning in the middle of June. I've been vomiting again, have just flushed my lost breakfast down the toilet, one blueberry still swirling stubbornly. I rally when she calls, I rally my son from his Legos, and we put on our socks and shoes and rain slickers to walk around Windmill Island.

Two days ago, we'd been at the beach with Nicole and her daughter, a dancer at a camp for young worship leaders facilitated in part by my husband. On Lake Michigan's shore, my son and I joined them for sub sandwiches on Lake Michigan's beachfront. Teens slap around a volleyball in their sweatshirts, a few cartwheel in the surf, a few, more brazen, scream as they dive headlong into the icy water, my husband and son right behind them, splashing and squealing, slowly turning blue with cold. Nicole and I can't even put our toes in, so we sink our feet ankle-deep in the sand and set about warming ourselves in the weak sun. She tells me Charleston's beaches are known for their sharks, so she doesn't take any chances. She stays away.

Sharks? Wow, I say. I wouldn't have guessed that about Charleston.

It's true, she laughs. Those sharks are not joking around and neither am I. No, thank you.

Well, zero sharks here in Michigan, I say, pulling in my shivering son to rub him dry with a fuzzy purple beach towel. Just hypothermia.

And Nicole laughs again, a light, filtering laugh, an easy laugh. She reaches out her hand and tucks closer the towel beneath my son's chin.

Nicole is hoping the weather will hold this week. She wants to see what there is to see in this town. So we make a list of places to go, most of the typical tourist spots I've never visited either, though I've lived in Holland a decade.

It's so muggy right now in Charleston, she says. This is kind of nice! As long as no one makes me swim.

Midweek we decide to brave the chance of rain and head to a tourist spot known for its fields of tulips, working windmill, and Dutch dancers. I pick her up from campus and she turns to greet my son, who waves shyly from the backseat. Soon, though, they're friends; Nicole is a teacher and asks all the right questions. By the time we park and pay our entrance fee, she knows more than she bargained for: his favorite Ninjago, the hardest part of being six, who in the family has the worst morning breath. What she doesn't know, because my son doesn't know to tell her, is that I'm seven weeks pregnant. That I've begun to puke with real conviction. That I'm gassy and thrilled and sleepless and starving and scared.

We walk Windmill Island, the tulips long gone but, in their stead, we ogle Klompen dancers in their blocky costumes and enormous horses wearily circling the sidewalks, the vast miniature turn-of-the-century Dutch village replete with running water in its channels. Along the way, my son asks questions of Nicole: what's her favorite restaurant, her favorite board game, what's her kids' names, their favorite colors, does the whole family dance for church like her daughter?

Oh, I let my daughter do the dancing, Nicole says, nobody wants to see *me* do that.

Across the lawn the canned strains of an organ overture signal another round of Klompen.

What Nicole doesn't tell my son is that her home church is now a tourist site, like the island we're walking about. That Emanuel AME is her church, Mother Emanuel. That her church has a long, hard, powerful history but also that last summer, nine of her friends were murdered there by a white boy with a pistol and a backpack full of bullets.

I watch my son ride the vintage merry-go-round, waving, while Nicole purchases a tiny pair of wooden shoes—keychain size—and a wedge of fudge dotted with walnuts. Soon it's too cold and rainy to do anything but take shelter inside the towering red and white windmill and wait for a tour. We sit on a huge slab of unfinished wood and my son buries his face in my armpit to get warm. I pull my jacket around him, and he tucks in further. I don't want him to hear what I'm going to say. I turn to Nicole and ask the question I've been trying out in my head all morning.

Is it good to get away?

She nods a little, sends out a breath through her teeth. She lifts her hands and gives a silent clap on each syllable: Yes, it is. She does that silent clap a couple more times, her nod slowly changing into a shaking of her head.

With a tiny lurch of horror, I realize I've just ruined the 'getting away.' I've slammed her again with a reminder not only of her reality, but the gaze of the voyeur.

We don't have to talk about it, I say, my lips pinched with shame, I shouldn't have asked.

But she's already speaking: Can you believe that tomorrow is the one-year anniversary?

She looks at me, blinking. I feel a streak of bile snake up the back of my throat. I swallow and taste salt.

When they return to Charleston, they've got a week's worth of emotionally draining days ahead. Long days, long week. Big shots, as she calls them, will fly in, make speeches, pose for the cameras, and fly out. The rest of them will be there to carry on, attend church each week and midweek.

That's why, she continues, she and her daughter are so glad to be in Michigan at this camp right now. They needed to get away. They needed to distract themselves, because they know what's waiting for them when they return.

My son wriggles against my ribs, but I find Nicole's hand. She takes in a rickety breath.

The night it happened, her daughter had dance practice, but she and her son had driven downtown and planned on being at church. First, though, her son had insisted on going shopping for a certain kind of button-up shirt for work, and he was so intent on finding the right one that they missed church altogether. She kept telling him they needed to go, that they could still make it to the Bible study, but he knew he'd find the exact shirt he needed in the next store. Just one more store. Just one more.

I try to hide it, but I'm shivering. I bend sideways slowly, my son burrowed in my arms, until my forehead is on Nicole's shoulder. I can speak nothing into this moment. She leans in, drapes her arm over my son's back.

And then a woman steps out from behind a desk and says, peppy as a lemon, It's time for the next tour! So we unfold ourselves. We stand and Nicole holds my sleepy son's hand up the narrow stairs. We nibble on wheat berries and marvel at the antiquated hooks and hammers and we ask questions of the milliner. We steady ourselves for another two flights up, my son holding me tighter and tighter the higher we go. On the top level of the windmill, shipped piecemeal from the Netherlands, we step cautiously onto a deck that looks out across the island, into the marshy bay of Macatawa, which feeds, eventually, to Lake Michigan. It's windy but not raining and seems as if we can see across hundreds of miles. Green and blue and more green and more blue.

***

The third baby we lose is a girl we name Havilah. She is the only lost baby with a diagnosis: Trisomy 22, which is, we're told, 'incompatible with life.' Though we'd kept the pregnancy a secret from my son, we decide to come out with all of it after I've returned from the hospital, after I'm up and able to piece together a puzzle with him. Dice a boiled egg for a snack.

Why did she die? he asks, twirling a slice of egg white on his finger.

Some babies are too sick to be born, I say, and they die very early, before they even begin to look or act like babies inside their mamas.

But why, he stops to think, popping the disc of yolk out of another slice, then replacing it. Why do so many of *our* babies die?

I shake my head. I shrug. It feels like someone's opened up the cupboard of my chest and slapped me across the heart. And yet it also spears up a small light, just a flicker, way down inside me. I've read something about this. I promise myself I'll return to it later.

He says, I've been praying for a baby sister. We could name her 'Flower.' Or even 'Snow Flower.' Let's pray again tonight. We can pray tomorrow, too.

I kiss him, his hair. The backs of his hands, his eyebrow. Snow Flower. What age-appropriate words, ideas, or images can I find to say that prayer is not enough? It didn't stop Dylann Roof. It doesn't save the Togolese. It didn't help Havilah.

Even as this thought flits through me, I sense I'm wrong, like I'm wrong about a lot of things. Or, if not wrong, not yet right. I won't know it for a while, but it might be that prayer's work is not about getting, but shaping. Maybe like the work of lament or protest: not making any one thing happen, necessarily, but creating space for the shape of longing, and suffering, and being shorn to the roots, for the budding and building of movement.

***

As we're losing Havilah, my sister also miscarries, a baby that's both conceived and then lost within days of my daughter. It's taken years for her to get pregnant again, and the timing, with malaria medications, is tricky. They're home in the Midwest on furlough, their plans shot through, so my sister and I speak daily, the connection clear and sharp, all our vowels ringing. One day she says, I think I understand a little better now.

Understand what?

All these years I've been practicing as a doctor, I didn't really get it. All the women and babies, she says. You, she says, almost whispering. I was sympathetic, but I didn't really *know*. I didn't have a clue.

I'm sorry, she says. And I realize it's not just Jericho, Tiernan, and Havilah, but every woman, every baby, from Togo to Tacoma to Holland and back, every ache that's rising in front of her like a mountain whose height each new experience must now proportionately reckon.

I know, I say, and together we sit, quiet on the line.

***

Three months after my sister and I lose our babies, much of (white) America is awakened to, or reminded of, its endemic backwardness by its willingness to elect a leader whose capital is creating fear of the other, commodifying human worth. My son and his father and I talk a lot about this, about bullies and power and who is valuable and why our neighbors and family have this man's signs in their yard, this man who makes Mama and Papa cry.

Should we not let him see us weep? Should we pretend this is only about differences in political ideals, of elephants and donkeys, and not the great caving in of a nation to its basest impulses, masked—with wicked insistence—as spirituality and fiscal responsibility?

My son and I go to the store and buy poster board and tape. We spread markers across the carpet. I ask him: what do you want to write on your sign? Maybe, 'We Love Immigrants and Refugees'? Or, 'Black Lives Matter'? Or, 'Women Are Not Objects'? With some stumbling—I have so far to go in recognizing and confronting my own privilege—I've used the most age-appropriate words, ideas, and images I can to help him understand why each of these messages are worth carrying when we march, even if marches are, in terms of function, a lot like prayer. He's been to silent vigils on campus, to meetings for mobilizing activists and allies, meetings to talk practicalities and logistics. He's raced around the basement with Ahmed, newly arrived from Afghanistan. He knows, I hope, that marching is but a place to begin.

He pulls the cap off a chunky permanent marker, sounding each word out: B-L-A-C-K (space) L-I-V-E-S (space) M-A-T-T-E-R. He changes the period to an exclamation point.

He says, All done! He looks at me and grins: Our time is now!

It is, I say, grinning back. He's parroting. He's heard this somewhere, but the pronoun jars my memory, that little flicker I meant to return to. Our babies. Our time.

It may be nothing. But it may be something, the start of, perhaps, what social psychologist Christena Cleveland calls The Power of Us. When we're involved with one another, Cleveland says, when we're connected to one another, our sense of self expands to include the other; research shows we'll share our resources as well as our pain, we'll forgive and be forgiven, we'll give the benefit of the doubt regarding ambiguous intentions and we'll stick our necks out for the other; we'll say 'yes' to being challenged in our worldviews and perceptions; we'll say 'yes' to being part of each other's stories.

I've messed up in multiple and myriad ways with age-appropriate issues. Still, here he is, a hot pink poster board in his hands. Here we are, our heels, our tongues slapping haplessly against the ancient power of *me*, of *mine*. Here we are, shuffling toward an *our*, an *us*.

What if instead of, *is he old enough for this,* the question could be, *who is ever too young?*

SATIN FLOWERS IN GRAVEYARDS

Jeff Newberry

These die, too. In spring storms of hail and wind,
in the sun's relentless burn. Even fake flowers fade.
    The florist downtown keeps a stock of funeral-ready
banners and bouquets: *In Remembrance, RIP,* crepe crosses—
    the rented grief you see after grave-side services
when only the tent remains. Somewhere,
    the left behind eat cold fried chicken and pretend
that everything tastes the same. My aunt set fake
    bouquets by my father's and uncle's graves for years
and years before death came for her, too. I miss
    the Styrofoam-bottomed plastic vases that once
littered the family plot. No one puts flowers there
    anymore. When I stand over these plain gray slabs,
grass grows up to the edge. I left a framed poem
    at my father's grave once. A week later, the rain
had bleached the paper white as though I'd never written a word.

AUBADE ON BLACK ROCK MOUNTAIN

Jeff Newberry

A morning chill grips the cabin, reminds
    me that in the end, I'm bone and body,
meat on a frame. What can die can rot.
    The pelt drying outside had been
a six-point yesterday morning. Even
    plant matter mulches. Roots drink
from the rot. I've boiled coffee and sip
    the black, grit my teeth against the morning
wind. An old man at church told me
    some Native American tribes imagined
hell an endless tundra of frozen soil.
    No food, no nothing. It was their
worst nightmare. Hell, then, must be
    the worst we can imagine. On this lonely
mountain, I can imagine anything.
    Outside, I study last night's campfire
ashes, consider the sweet gum and pines
    consumed by fire. I sat up late looking
for patterns in the sky. Ancient sailors
    did the same, I've read—traced meaning
into the stars' chaos. Only one remains fixed,
    though, the North Star, while the rest whirled
like the fiery wheels Van Gogh saw. I kneel
    now by the fire pit and run my fingers
through ashes, snatch my hand away.
    Somewhere in the gray, a spark remains.

WHAT I THINK IT WILL BE LIKE TO BE MARRIED TO YOU

Meredith Stewart Kirkwood

like having an angel to wrestle with
in the years of my life, those unknown plains
stretching to death's horizon—
an angel who will touch my hip
cause me pain, bless me.
I have been wrestling too long
with the sky
synapses pulsing in my head
threads of dreams and younger versions
of myself. But it's you
I want now, the real, tangible—
the you who looks at me with dinner plate eyes
of disbelief when I break down
and cry on the floor.
The you who sits next to me.

That's what I think it will be like to be married to you:
reading a book, say *The Little Prince*, over and over
and underlining a different passage every time—
every time the music of the words in my head
the shape of each letter attended to
because I have that much time
and it's the only book I'm reading
this life.

Like memorizing the shifting light on my lawn
the grass tall or short
the season winter or fall
the arch of the sun, the interruption
of dandelion or sowthistle.
Maybe it's summer, maybe spring
each new shifting light the glint new
in your blue iris. My chest

rising and falling with the glint, the grass growing.
I will memorize you, each blade
and when you change I will start again—

THE SHELL

Laura Arciniega

There was once a woman who gave birth to her child. Laying him in his cradle, she smoothed his golden curls and tied on her apron. She brought out a bowl, a spoon, and some flour. She neither measured nor levelled. Her hands flew as she stirred and poured. Soon there was an enormous mound of dough before her, dull-colored and sticky and lightly bubbling. Without forming it, she placed the dough, still in the bowl, into the hot oven. Then she lay down to sleep.

Her child had been secretly watching her. He was surprised that she put the bowl in the oven and determined to ask her about it when she woke. Meantime, he watched the oven. It had started rumbling and shaking the minute his mother had closed the door. Now sparks of light were escaping from around the door's edges, blue, the bluest you've ever seen. His mother had mentioned that their home stood on a spit of land that jutted out into a sea—could the blue of the sparks be the blue of the sea?

Suddenly it all stopped. The woman rose from her bed and went to the oven. She opened the door and reached in. Her child cried out; he was afraid that his mother would burn her hands.

"Don't worry, my love," she said, as she brought out a pan with three golden loaves.

At this her child marveled even more. His mother tidied the kitchen and, lifting her child from the cradle, said, "Do you have something to ask me, my love?"

"Yes, Mama," said the child, speaking his first words. "Why did you put the bowl in?"

"Oh, my love, you'll learn that many things can be done like that," his mother said.

"Oh," said her child. "But you didn't form the dough?"

"No, no, I didn't. Most things don't need my help. I do very little, you'll see. And one day you'll do very little as well."

"Oh. Are you angry with me, Mama?"

"My sweet one, why would I be angry with you?"

"I pretended to be asleep."

"Well, I don't like to be at odds with you. I'd rather you slept when I think you're asleep, but I'm not angry."

The child smiled and touched his mother's hair. The woman touched his nose and they laughed together for a while. Then the woman nursed him and he went to sleep truly.

When the woman's husband came home, he put down his bag, kissed his wife, and took their child from her arms. The child woke instantly. Delighted to see his father, he cried out, "Daddy!"

The man smiled. "So he's talking, then?"

"Well, he is three," his wife answered.

"You've got a point there. Did you make the bread?"

"I did."

"Good. They're on their way." To his child he said, "Come with Daddy and I'll teach you to play the kithara."

His wife laughed. "They don't call it that anymore."

"Ha! The vihuela, then. Let's go."

All that evening, the family talked and laughed, ate and played. When it was time for bed, the child asked for a story.

His father began, "Far away, there is a place where the day passes so slowly that a hen knows she's about to lay an egg before she lays it, and whales can hear the whaling boats coming before they've arrived."

"It's nothing like here!" the child said.

"No," his mother agreed, "nothing at all. Trees bud and flower for whole seasons, not just for moments. And a thing called 'rain' happens there."

"What is it like?" asked the child.

His father said, "It's like puddles, but slower. And in that place, children go for years without being able to do much that people do here. They cannot even walk or talk for a long time."

"Are the people there bored? What do they do all day, if things take so long?"

"They think and worry. They plan and change plans and wait with great difficulty. They have so much time that they are fooled into thinking that they can control it."

"But," said the child, "shouldn't they be happy? They can enjoy things with all that time."

"Yes, they should be happy. We are happy here, even though our moments pass so quickly that a person can't do or say or expect much of anything; time is a great gift and it is a good thing to have even a little of it."

Then, as it was almost dawn, the family slept. When they woke a few minutes later, they ate and the father left for the day.

"If I remember correctly, I believe they'll be here by noon," he said as he closed the door.

"I believe you're right," answered his wife, and she kissed him quickly before he was gone.

Just before noon, while the woman and her child were playing and running through the house, someone knocked. The woman took her child's hand and they opened the door.

Two youths stood there, panting and dressed in tatters. The young man spoke.

"Excuse me, ma'am. We've run out of food. Can you offer us anything? We would be grateful."

"Yes, come in," the woman answered.

The young man and the young woman took their seats at the table. The woman's child brought them cups of water and the woman brought out the pan with the three golden loaves.

"Oh, no," they cried, "we couldn't possibly eat anything now! We are already full as it is from this water."

"Of course not. This bread is for your camels," said the woman. "Let's go out to them now." And they all rose.

The day was beautiful; the sun was strong and bright and a cool breeze blew every now and then, rustling every nook and cranny of the world. The prairie grasses swayed right down the bluff.

Twelve Bactrians stood in the road. Anyone could see that they were thirsty.

"How long has it been since they drank?" the woman asked. She set the loaves on the ground and the camels began to move towards them, nosing through the grass.

The young woman began to cry as she said, "Over a year."

"We cannot thank you enough, but our camels do not eat, and they drink only saltwater," said the young man. "The sea here—is it saltwater?"

"No, it is fresh, but it is a peculiar body of water. I baked these loaves with it and it will quench their thirst."

The child and the young couple saw that it was true: as the camels consumed the loaves, their appearance improved. Their coats and eyes brightened, and their sagging skin fattened up.

The young woman turned to the young man and murmured, "Will they need to chew the cud of this bread?"

"This food is not like the food that camels eat," said the woman's child. The young couple looked at him in surprise, for they suddenly noticed that he was taller than he had been when he had served their water.

"No?" they asked.

"No, I suspect it is more easily digested, though it is sturdier. If they finish this bread, they should not need to eat again for a decade." He looked up at his mother. "At least."

She nodded in agreement. "Let's go down to the beach," she said, taking the child's hand.

The women led the way through the tall grass. The wind brushed past them and went west. When they reached the sand, they took off their shoes and felt it warm and satin under their feet. The child ran towards the water.

"This place is beautiful. How long have you lived here?" asked the young woman. She picked up a piece of white driftwood, small and thin and smooth as a flute.

"Oh, a long, long time," answered the woman. "About four years."

The young woman and young man looked very confused. "But four years isn't a long time at all!" the young woman said.

The woman smiled and looked out at the sea. Her son was walking in the tiny waves that came just to his ankles. It was not a happy smile, exactly, but it was not sad, either; it was a smile of knowing and accepting something for just what it was. "Here, it is," she said.

The child came running back, a shell in his hand. "Look!" he cried, breathless. His golden hair was tossed all over his head. He held up the shell for them all to see. It was a tan and cream disk dosinia.

"Ah," said the young man, "we have shells like that at home, don't we?"

"Yes," said the young woman. She slipped the driftwood into her pocket and pulled a chain from the neck of her blouse. On it was a disk dosinia.

The child's eyes widened. "It's the same shell!" he shouted.

"Well, they are similar," the young couple agreed.

"No," said the woman. "It is the same shell. Put them together."

Baffled, the young woman took her necklace off and unthreaded the disk dosinia from it. She took the shell from the child's hand and laid it on top of her own. They interlocked at the hinge. They were not similar; they were the same.

The young couple looked at each other, frightened; they looked at the woman.

"Please don't be afraid," she said. "My husband will be home soon. Let's go back now and meet him."

It was a golden four or five o'clock and the sun ran on the sea and on the grass and on the child's golden head as the four of them ascended the bluff. When they reached the house, they heard a "Hello!" from behind them. It was the woman's husband, running toward them and smiling. "Hello! Hello," he said, shaking hands with the young couple. "I'm so glad you've come. Will you stay awhile?"

"Yes, thank you, that's very kind," they said.

The man beamed. "Wonderful. Shall I cook tonight?" he asked his wife.

"Let's cook together," she answered. And they went inside.

The young couple sat on the floor as the child talked. He walked back and forth in a half-moon around them, gesticulating and lifting his eyebrows and sometimes shouting as he described the wonder of the birds and the animals and the sea in the place he lived. The young woman gave him the driftwood flute from the beach and he became even more buoyant.

"This is a gemshorn," he told them.

They did not know what he was talking about but they were rapt at his exuberance. His parents sliced and seasoned and braised and blackened in the kitchen. They made a homey clatter of wooden spoons and dishes and pots. Though they did not speak much as they cooked, they smiled often. Once, the husband asked, "Do they know?" to which his wife said, "No." And once she said, "I love you," and her husband responded, "I love you, too."

After a few moments, they laid a feast on the table and everyone sat down to eat.

The young man said, "Your son found a shell on the beach and it was the other half of the shell my wife wears on a necklace. How could that be?"

The husband sighed. He seemed reticent to say much. "This place—our home here on the sea—is special. It is different in a way that is difficult to explain."

The young couple frowned and went on eating. The child asked them about their home.

"It is dry and hot there. There are towering mountains and trees that stretch above the clouds. There are all kinds of desert animals and birds. It is a wonderful place!" the young woman said. She was young, so she said this with all the liveliness and naiveté of youth.

"How long have you been married?"

"Only four years."

"What is time like there?" asked the child.

"What do you mean?" the young man asked.

"How long do things take?"

"Oh, they take the usual length of time," said the young woman slowly. "Is it different here?"

"Oh, yes. Have you not noticed it?" said the child.

"Well, I suppose we have," said the young woman, looking around. It was dark outside. They had missed the sunset entirely.

The young man looked down at his plate. It was bare, though he'd only taken three bites.

The woman turned to her child and said, "My love, would you please clear away the dishes?"

"Yes, Mama."

Once he was in the kitchen, the woman turned to the young couple and said, "Does this place not feel familiar?"

The young woman put her hand to her shell necklace. The young man looked hard at her and opened his mouth to speak. He said nothing for a few strained moments, and then he said, "Have we? I mean, have we been here before?"

"You have," answered the man. "A long time from now."

The young woman was pale. "I remember," she murmured, her voice cracking.

"It's alright," the woman said to her. "It's alright."

The young woman's eyes were wide. "But your hair is white." She spoke so quietly that the others could barely hear her.

"So is yours, now," said the woman. She put her hand on the young woman's shoulder.

Shocked at these words, the young man looked at his wife. Their faces were filled with terror. The child returned from the kitchen.

Only he wasn't a child anymore. He stood several feet taller than when he'd left the table. He was now a young man.

The young couple stared.

"Here is the cake, and here are the plates," he said as he laid everything out.

"Thank you," said his father, smiling gratefully.

The cake was eaten in silence, taking hardly a moment, and then the young couple was shown to the guest room.

The man and woman sat on their bed and wondered if they'd said too much too soon. What they had revealed was not the sort of thing that could be told too early; it had to be gradually realized by the hearer first before anyone could speak up to explain. Even so, they could hear the young woman clarifying everything to the young man, who kept exclaiming, "What?" in a voice he thought was a whisper. They were worried that their son would hear also, but for now they could tell from the light snoring that he was asleep. Finally, they lay down as well, resolved that they had done the best they could.

After an hour, the sun rose again and the air was fresh and alive with summer. Everyone met at the table for breakfast. The young man who had been a child went out to feed the camels.

"Are you alright?" the woman asked the young couple. There were lines at the corners of their eyes and mouths, and they looked tired. The young man's hair had begun to go gray. In fact, they were not a young couple anymore. They now resembled their hosts.

"Yes," they breathed, "yes, we are."

"I see now, and I've accepted it all," said the man who used to be young.

"What will happen now?" asked the woman who used to be young. "What do we do?"

"It will all come to you very naturally," answered the woman, the mother. "You do not have to do much. Just live." She smiled. "The worst part is over now. Well, the second-worst part."

"Tomorrow, you will have the baby," said her husband. "And that will be the hardest part."

"Giving birth?" asked the woman who used to be young.

"No," he said, looking at his wife. "Seeing him grow up in just a day or so. Being powerless to slow time."

"We remember what it was like where we used to live, where you came from," said his wife. "We remember how long things used to take. It was a gift. I see that now." The couple who had been young nodded.

The young man who had been a child came back into the house and his mother said, "Now, let's have something to eat."

"Mama," he said a few minutes later, as the two of them washed up after breakfast, "they look very much like you and Dad, don't you think?"

"Yes, the same," she said.

"Hmmm," he said. "Mother?"

"Yes?"

"I love you." He embraced her. She remembered the tiny grasping embrace of her baby, his arms clinging to her as she cradled him, just a day or so ago.

"I love you, too." Her voice was steady despite her tears.

***

The old man and old woman stood hand in hand looking at the sea. The sun was behind them. The afternoon air was so still that the sea appeared nearly frozen, as in winter. Seagulls complained on the rocks near the shore. The old woman handed the old man, her husband, a piece of chocolate and she ate a piece herself.

"Thank you," he said.

"You're welcome. Isn't this the most beautiful day?"

"Yes. I don't think I've seen lovelier."

"I didn't think we would always live here."

"Neither did I. Things turned out differently than I expected. But our clothes have no holes and our feet are without bruises."

"And have you been happy?" she asked.

"No," he said darkly.

The old woman gasped.

"Yes! Yes, I've been happy! Of course I have," said her husband. He was laughing.

"That's not funny," she said.

"Don't be angry. It was very funny."

"I'm not angry. I haven't been angry for years."

"Good," he said, still smiling.

They stood in silence a little longer. Then the old woman said, "Finish your chocolate and let's go back."

"I'm glad you're not angry," said her husband.

"So am I," she replied as they turned to walk home.

When they got near the house, a child came running out to meet them.

"Grandma! Grandpa!" she cried with abandon. She leapt up and the old man caught her in his arms.

"Here you go, my love," said the old woman, handing the child a piece of chocolate.

"Thank you!" she said.

"You are very welcome, my dear."

The child reached into her pocket and took out the driftwood flute. "Here you go, Grandma. You take the gemshorn."

"Why, thank you. We should probably call it a kaval now." The old woman put it into her pocket and looked at her husband. "You didn't ask if *I've* been happy."

"Well?"

"Oh, yes. I have been happier than I thought possible. How could you even ask that?"

A man came out of the house as they approached. "Dinner is ready," he announced.

The old man, the old woman, their son, daughter-in-law, and grandchild ate and talked late into the evening. After a few moments, the daughter-in-law said, "We have news."

The old man and the old woman said, "Oh?" though they had already guessed and knew they would never see the child.

"We will have a baby in the spring," she said. The child clapped.

"That is wonderful news," said the old man.

"Congratulations! How are you feeling?" said the old woman.

The daughter-in-law took a deep breath and closed her eyes. "Terrible," she said with an enormous smile.

They all laughed and the old woman said, "I'm sorry to hear that. What do you need?"

"Nothing right now, thank you."

"What about dessert? To celebrate?" asked her husband. He winked.

The daughter-in-law—and everyone else—admitted that dessert was a propos, so the old woman and her son went to the kitchen. While they were collecting the cutlery and the dishes, the old woman said, "You have made us all so happy." Her son smiled and put his hand on her shoulder, and then they brought out the cake.

A moment later and everyone was going to bed. The old man and the old woman turned out the light and lay down in their room. "Thank you," said the old man.

"For what?" asked his wife, turning towards him.

"For everything. I *have* been happy."

They smiled in the dark, and they went to sleep for the last time.

SALT

James Allman, Jr.

You are the salt of the earth. But if the salt loses its saltiness it is no longer good for anything,
except to be thrown out and trampled underfoot.
—Jesus, from the sermon "Salt and Light" (Matthew 5:13-16)

From PIE *sal-, where we get the word for 'soldier'—*sal dare,* 'to give salt
    to', or
earn one's salt, which is how they were paid in those days—if
Pliny the Elder is to be believed.

And they are plentiful, now, and everywhere. And they salt the earth
with their boot-soles—soldiers sent to the four corners. As if a common
misinterpretation of Jesus' words occurred—chieftains and
heads of state taking seriously a godly burden to season everything

sufficiently. And the soldiers, before ever they will be
beaten into ploughshares eons from now, dig their swords in and turn
them—sowing fields with their salinity. Singing:

We are the salt and the light and we do not salt lightly. Salty as
sailors we are, we are the salt sent away to give
the sea its brine. We are pillars of salt on sortie assailing what is not Kosher with
teaspoons. We draw lines. We hold them.
We have many followers. We are turned loose afield and no field is left fallow

of us. Which is the *hal-* of it. Salt, or sea-salt. Or the ceaselessness of
sea. As in the sea will always have its own way—its way
being halcyon. Of the sea—or of itself—even if tempestuous. And a cruel
    mistress.
The surf—the incessant
lapping of its salt-lick against the sand. The sand—a thin
line of peeling scab tended by seaweed salves and hermit crabs

and beach goers. Gawking with beach towels. And beach chairs and
trowels and beach umbrellas. Resting on beached
asses. Their crucifixes buried

in chest hairs. Deep as beach grasses. And maybe they're languishing

with picnic baskets, copper mules of sweet tea, and a dash
of salt in their chocolate chip cookies. Like the gentrified gathered on the
      lawn
in their Sunday's best
to watch the First Battle of Bull Run. Or that stretch
of sand might be Thermopylae. All that stands between. The Devil and the
      deep blue sea.

WHAT SHE MUST SEE

Sarah Davis

She is almost fifteen.

The door closes on a peeking piece of a mother wearing all black Christopher and Banks. Mom's necklace alternates little silver balls and black oblong beads. Clinique fuchsia-pink lipstick freshly applied. Sensible black Sketchers in a subtle attempt to be comfortable and ordinary. I can imagine her packing them, in careful preparation for a lot of downtown Chicago walking.

The door shuts and Sketcher footsteps squeak away. Muffled politeness declines a water.

The girl's composite card is professional enough. Basic font choice—Arial maybe. Two outfits, four pictures. 5'9" and size two, sure, but the hips are at a risky 35.

Black V-neck cause someone told her to. Cheap black heels and dark wash skinny jeans of course. Hair is reddish blonde to the root and in a mess of natural kinks, early morning barrel curls by an untrained hand. The curls are not in her face, but she tucks them behind her ear. She stoops slightly from years of unaware hunching, meeting the heights of sundress friends who never showed too much thigh in church.

Her legs are sticks like everyone's. Freckles skip across her face, some spots bigger than others. Eyes, bright hazel behind a nervous coat of mascara—maybe from the Clinique cosmetic gift bag mom got when she bought the fuchsia-pink. She looks up to meet our eyes, shifting to stand a little straighter, to seem a little stronger than she feels. Not too strong though. Just the right amount of strong.

She is almost fifteen.

"Hi," she smiles and tucks her hair again. Her teeth are off-white virgin bones that have not yet met the white strip. She scans the room. What she must see.

We sit at one large, rectangle table that fills the space to her right. To her left is a tiny box dressing room with a curtain door. Floating shelves line the modern brick wall behind us—displaying comp cards all better than hers, with matching fonts and pictures. An exhibit of the few, for the few. The Elite. Faces and bodies.

"Hi." We serve her greeting back to her with generous fake smiles. She eats them quickly. I wonder how sick she'll be if she doesn't slow down.

"How are you today?" Kelly asks with professionalism and feigned interest. I hate Kelly.

"I'm good," she answers too perkily, realizing it after the words escape her mouth and then squeezing her shoulders in a little more. She grips her portfolio book in front of her and holds it out over our table. "I have this…" she says awkwardly.

"You can set it there," Kelly says easily, surveying the girl's card. She motions to the corner of the table.

The girl puts down the book and hates not having something to hold. The corner of the table is too far for anyone to reach. We will not look at it; it does not matter. It is apparent she does not yet have the experience worth our time. How could she at almost fifteen? It occurs to me she has other experiences. But we are too worthy to ever know them. We do not reach.

"You have a bikini?" another member of the table asks.

"Yes," she answers, quick and responsible. She is straight A's, I'm sure. And she is hopeful, but probably secret keeping. This is just another fun weekend with Mom. She already did all her homework; they will go to dinner, shop but not buy anything, stay in a hotel—Hampton Inn maybe—and be home Sunday night by 8pm. On Sunday morning dad will tell curious congregation members it's just a fun girl's weekend. He knows and disapproves of it all. "I guess we'll see what happens," he says to them at home. He is probably secret keeping too—his pride.

"It's on under my clothes."

"Great. The dressing room is to your left and make sure to keep the heels on."

She nods, tucks more curls, and dives into the dressing room desperate to escape all the eyes. In the little closet with velvet curtain, I imagine she breathes for the first time in two minutes. She pulls her shirt up over her curls and peels off her jeans to reveal a black two-piece that will never swim. Never see the sun—only the glow of agency lamps and digital camera flashes.

She doesn't want to take too long. She squares her shoulders, maybe cocks her chin up. Smiles. Purses lips. What do they want? Personality, but not too much. Professional, but act your age. Underweight, but not anorexic. Tall, but not freakish. Pretty, but not gorgeous. Natural, but flawless. Just look like yourself, but god forbid you don't look like everyone else.

She thinks she's been in there too long now. Combs fingers through hair, flips it, combs again. Hands on hips. New bruise? Never mind. Combs again. Small smile. Okay. She sucks in a ghost-white stomach and breathes it out. Runs bone hands over a body that is almost fifteen.

Click-click, heels on tired wood. A pale arm parts the velvet curtain and she steps out in all the awkward elegance of a 5'10" junior high girl. We all look. Up, down. And I hate the habit of my eyes.

"Could you walk for us?" Kelly breathes coolly.

"Of course," she eats.

More clicking and it is nearly deafening. Echoing pounding. Across from me she strides to the far brick on my left, brushing the backs of swivel chairs—trendy bald heads and wanting women in their early-thirties.

One hand on hip at the end of the makeshift runway. She waits three seconds in perfect count with feet in the T-shape. Turns around. Sashays back too fast in the euphoric confidence of pure pretending.

"Great. Now could you spin slowly for us?" A question that is not a question. She obeys. A small red line is above her stomach where the folds of a natural belly meet when you sit. Maybe the line appeared in the taxi on the way here. Or maybe it's from earlier that morning, sitting in an all white bed and trying to figure out how to get a taxi to the Hampton Inn. Either way, the line is there and she is a human girl.

She is fourteen.

"Okay, that's all. Thank you so much," Kelly says. "We'll keep you on file."

She tucks hair again, takes her book and thanks us with straight-A politeness. She smiles briefly in relief. She doesn't know the curse of the red stomach line. Her hesitant mascara lashes flash a final naïve attempt to read the room.

She doesn't know my turmoil and she doesn't know hers yet. I wish she could hear the dumb screaming confession of my eyes, but she only smiles, tucks hair, opens the door.

Pounding new heel-clicks close in on the entry.

I wonder if she could forget. And I wonder if forgetting could include forgiving the obscure faces above ties and blazers that leave you naked for years. But the door closes now, behind another elegant and awkward . . . In front of another peeking and straining . . .

"Hi."

A new one tucks her hair. I hear muffled politeness decline a water.

IT WASN'T ODD

Rachel E. Hicks

Last night I dreamed my elderly neighbor
sought me out, found me upstairs in my bedroom.
Miz Dinty—her trademark black baseball cap,
gold-crowned teeth flashing a grimace this time,

not her mischievous smile—climbed into the bed
I had just vacated in surprise, remarked
on its warmth in the early light. I'm dying,
she said, shivering. It's coming now, baby.

I hovered, then climbed in beside her,
wrapped my arms around her, whispered
how do you know? Maybe I didn't ask
her aloud. She just breathed in, then out.

Because it was a dream it wasn't odd
that the two of us lay there warming,
silent, unafraid. That I wanted this
to be how she was ushered on.

JUST BEFORE

Rachel E. Hicks

When Jesus comes again
in all his glory, somewhere in the Sichuan mountains
tires will crackle over corn
spread out on the road—
easy threshing—while a small child
urinates in the gutter, absorbed
in watching the car shoot by

As the first rent opens
a fingernail tear in the hazy sky
a woman in the foothills above Rishikesh
will lay down her firewood burden
and light the clay Diwali lamp
in the chilling dusk
circling her cupped hands in blessing

In the pause before the clamor
of heaven's trumpets
the jurors' waiting room in Baltimore's
civic court will throb with the quiet
turning of pages, a buzzing phone
in the hand of a tired man, berating
himself for forgetting to bring coffee

Just before we are aware of him
Jesus will pause to survey the view
two shepherd boys amidst boulders
in the Wadi Rum hills outside Amman
wipe sleep from their eyes and stand amazed
at the blood-red poppies at their feet
stretching to the eastern horizon

YOU'LL KNOW WHEN IT'S READY

Tania Runyan

I've taken to baking bread
without a machine, like a teenager
learning to dance from scratch.
Just swirl and float to the music,
baby, like a lavender
wisp of smoke. Just walk

your fingers through the dough, walk
until the shape of bread
appears in your hands like lavender
fields appeared in the teenaged
dreams of Monet. My kid osmosed music
hiding between the scratches

of a vinyl record. A ghost bass scratched
out its melancholy walk
outside of time, outside of music's
charts and bars. But I was bred
to follow directions. As a teenager
I paired pink with lavender

because only pink and lavender
lived in harmony. I scratched
out algebraic tasks like a teenaged
trained chicken. I tallied the cross walk's
flashes as countdown to my death. My bread,
today, rises like crescendoing music

in the dark, the yeasty music
of everything I've never leavened or
allowed to go free, like this bread
that I threw together from scratch
without stopping to walk
back to the recipe. Now my teenager

rips off a hunk of bread with a teenaged
flourish, hunger and music
propelling her kitchen-bedazzling walk.
I dedicate her to russet and lavender
scarves, to writing without scratching
out her words, to baking spontaneous bread.

I took a walk with my teenager.
We devoured fresh bread like music,
danced in the lavender dusk without a scratch.

SESTINA FOR FLU SEASON

Tania Runyan

The doctor's office staggers like a drunken masquerade,
faces obscured by Insta-Gard flu masks and shoulders
lurching to the rhythm of coughs. *Ninety minutes*
is ridiculous! wails a man with two hearing aids,
and I fold myself into the timeless envelope
of waiting. I'm just here for the lab to draw my blood.

Behind white doors people lay out their arms for blood
pressure cuffs, stand on scales, and masquerade
as immortals. Nurses fold results into envelopes
as doctors toss stethoscopes over their shoulders
between strep tests and hockey stitches, the first-aid
procedures of suburbia. *How many more minutes*

can I wait? the deaf man yells every few minutes,
and an old woman's face simmers with the blood
of annoyance. *Jesus,* she mutters, and I come to the aid
of all the maligned and broken hearted, the masquerade
ball of grotesqueries we carry on our shoulders.
I catch the old woman's gaze, envelop

her in smug compassion, and push my envelope:
he's deaf, I mouth, and point to my ear with a minute
gesture that causes her to twitch her shoulders
with rage. Sitting with strangers is a crapshoot of love, a blood
sport of grace, an unspoken masquerade
too embarrassed to live out Facebook's touching visual aids:

ruffians dancing together on subways, adorable AIDS
orphans from *shithole countries* enveloping
themselves in afghans crocheted by gossips. I masquerade.
I smile without teeth. I pretend I don't care about the minutes
that pass as I wait for the phlebotomist to take my blood,
label two vials, and place a gloved hand on my shoulder:

You did great today! Like a kindergartener, I shoulder
her touch with a sloppy grin. The man with hearing aids
coughs and yells, *I was next!* his words blurring with the blood
on the hands that have struck him down. He's an envelope
stuffed with flu and misunderstandings, or worse, silent minutes
of invisibility. Or maybe he's an average ass in masquerade.

The woman hunches her shoulders and growls to Jesus again, the envelope
of her flu mask aiding and abetting the stifled minutes
of waiting. I hold a cotton ball against the blood and masquerade.

THE IRRITABLE WOMAN:
SOME THOUGHTS ON MOTHERING,
PRIDE, AMBITION AND DESPAIR

D.L. Mayfield

I think about men, who for so long got to claim grumpiness as a virtue. My own grandfather, who I knew as both a generous and meticulous man, was legendarily irritable when my father was growing up. This grandfather, born into a humble farming family, became an important and highly intelligent engineer working in the space program. Life revolved around him and his needs: the food he liked, the volume of noise he required, the places he had to move to in order to keep moving up in his position.

I think of my father-in-law, consumed by quiet anger, his wife and four children orienting their lives to suit his needs, his brooding, his sense of being wronged by the world.

I think about Don Draper, cracking open a beer when he had to be at home with his children, rushing off to the office every chance he could get.

Busy, important men, who could not seem to switch into the roles of nurturing, engaged caregivers when they needed to.

I think about these men, and I think about me in the mornings. Trying to drink my coffee in peace, trying to practice prayer and meditation and yoga and journaling in those first few moments of the day. Trying to harness my anxious and apocalyptic thoughts into a presentable state, trying so hard not to feel like it is the end of the world.

And then I think about my children, bounding into my room, eager to start a day that for them is only about possibility, newness, about sucking the very marrow from life—how many snacks can they get away with eating? How many books can they get a loving adult to read them? What discoveries will my daughter make in second grade? What will Elmo say to my son that makes him feel warm and seen, giggly and curious? They try and sit on my lap or snuggle up close to me, they spill my coffee and make silly faces in the mirror in my bedroom. They make each other cry, they make each other scream out silly songs.

I smile tightly, wishing I could be alone. They smile broadly, wishing to never leave my sight.

***

For Valentine's day, my husband got me a novelty mug. It was Bob from *Bob's Burgers*, pinching the bridge of his nose and closing his eyes with a grimace. The bold black text read, "I love you, but you're all terrible." It made me laugh.

A few days later I was drinking out of it when my 6 year old niece, who had spent the night, read the words aloud:

"I love you, but you're all terrible" she said slowly, her small face scandalized.

My daughter, a year older, explained it brusquely.

"Oh, that's just how my mom is. She's really grumpy in the mornings."

I tried to smile but felt hurt at how I had been summed up. After everything I do—cooking, cleaning, getting kids to school, finding socks that don't feel tight or scratchy, making sure we are all well fed and rested and get where we need to be—this is my legacy? I am the irritable one. The parent the children are slightly afraid of. The one who spends too much time inside of their head, annoyed when life interrupts in. I am composing essays while I wipe shitty bums, I am checking the news on my phone during bedtime reading breaks, I am listening to podcasts while I cook dinner. I am the one, I slowly realized, who thinks she is more important than everyone else.

***

Billy Graham had an emotionally distant dad. Graham was America's most famous evangelist, because he was so successful at what he did. One of the reasons why so many flocked down the aisles at his revivals was the juxtaposition of messages that seem incompatible: that God loves you, and that God will condemn you to a life of eternal torment unless you acknowledge and serve Him.

In his book *A Gentler God: Breaking Free of the Almighty*, Dough Frank highlights how Graham portrays God, especially in his earlier sermons, as both loving and also as an "impatient, quick-tempered, rigid and rejecting" father, speaking to his own upbringing with an imperfect parent. Graham's father asserted himself using a wide leather belt and, Frank points out, " . . . never could understand anyone who wanted to do anything other than physical labor . . . never played a game in his life, never cared about hunting or fishing or baseball or anything like that."

Doug Frank himself is the son of an evangelist. He has spent his life studying the men who have shaped American evangelicalism. He believes that it was because of their fraught relationships with their fathers that they found no disconnect in the "emotionally jarring" portraits of God they presented. A God bound by holiness, and not love.

Frank, like so many, began to doubt this ordering of the world when he had his own children. He could not imagine being separated from them for eternity, nor punishing them infinitely for finite actions. And if he was just a human, how could God not also love God's children all the more?

***

My husband wakes up when the toddler starts yelling. I can hear him scoop our blonde-haired son out of the crib and take him into the kitchen. I can hear him making oatmeal with blueberries, grinding coffee and boiling water. My daughter emerges from her room and heads down the hallway, opening cupboards and getting cereal for herself. She will have a graphic novel under her arm, and she will read while she slowly eats at the table, her hair wild from a night of deep and dreamless sleep.

I get a few precious moments to myself in bed in the dark while they are eating, busy, minds consumed. I wake up before everyone else, but I am not ready to face them. The thoughts I have in the morning are the same thoughts I have every day, the ones I fell asleep thinking about. *The world is fucked. Everything is terrible. I need to do something to fix it. Whatever I do will no doubt not work. But I have to do something. Because everything is so incredibly bad.*

The content doesn't matter, and changes by the day. The imminent end of DACA, our local affordable housing crisis, the dire and dropping refugee resettlement numbers, reports of mass casualties in the Syrian crisis, global warming, the NRA, Wall Street, famous evangelists stumping for a border wall along Mexico, neighbors who can't find a job, domestic violence, school inequality, and on and on and on.

I think about the problems, their complexities, how they affect people I love dearly. I think about how I feel powerless to do anything about any of it, and yet I know I must try. It's an endless loop of bad news and I am bound to it all. On the days I can't stop thinking about all the problems of the world, it is like going through life underwater, in a muffled state. Trying hard to hear my children and my husband, to process their needs and wants and desires even as my brain is living in another country, another world, one that is constantly ending.

***

What made so many men such bad dads? What made them go through life one step away from an explosion, or turn and twist themselves into a series of small implosions? Why did so many of their spouses and partners and children accept it, placate it, orient their lives around the anger and irritability that radiated out of men?

Augustine said that it was pride which made angels into devils. Pride harms others because of how it makes us operate in the world. There is the stereotypical way: the irritable dads in buttoned-down shirts, carrying briefcases—the ones who made the money and perhaps thought everything else was owed to them. Perhaps they believed they were more important than the other members of their family. Maybe they swallowed the philosophies of capitalism and consumerism, that the one who produces is the most valuable.

But then there are those who are harder to pick out, their brains hiding behind a smooth mask. At some point they get very, very tired from running through every possible problem they were confronted with, and what they were supposed to do about it. They think they are helping the world, but in reality they are just indulging in a deadly sin: The belief that the world rests on their shoulders, that they alone can do something about it. That if they stop thinking about the cares of the world for even a moment, it will all come crashing down and somehow be even worse than it already is.

They construct for themselves a world in which they are a god, and everyone else is a mere mortal.

***

I think about Billy Graham's dad, and how he shaped his son, who grew up to influence millions of people. I think about Bob from *Bob's Burgers*, how he's portrayed as a loveable and involved parent, despite his near-constant state of exasperation. I think about myself, trying to advocate for equitable schools by creating a petition for the superintendent and then snapping at my son when he dumps sand all over my freshly-swept floor. I am a mother, a neighbor, a friend. I am also an irritable woman.

Billy Graham wanted to convert the world. Bob wanted to make amazing burgers. My grandfather wanted to soar beyond the confines of the fields of wheat and sunflowers to the literal edges of the known universe.

I know I am a hard person to be friends with, to be married to, to have as a mother.

"You aren't a bad mother," my husband tells me. "You are just a values-driven person."

He means that I am obsessed with what I owe the world, while other people maybe do not do this every second of the day. I know my thoughts, I know they are a form of ambition, they are a form of pride. I want to save the world, which means that deep down I think I can.

My husband thinks my grumpiness in the morning is cute. How the kids climb all over me while I sigh inwardly with despair at all the work there is to be done. My husband listens to music in the morning, usually Ke$ha or Taylor Swift, whistling along. His own dad was not a very good one, and this sometimes makes him sad. He takes care of our children in a way that is more detached but pleasant: tuning out their incessant requests, not bothering to investigate screams unless they sound *really* bad, playing mundane board games over and over again. I am the highly invested parent, the one always asking questions and listening to stories, the one answering every question the second it is asked, buying the books I know they will love.

My children know this about me. They cling to me every second they can get. We live together in an emotionally jarring world, we are trying to reconcile what we value and how we treat each other. How to live in the world and absorb the sorrows within without it killing you. Learning to pay attention to simple joys like peanut butter pretzels or unexpected snow days or re-reading a book for the millionth time.

My children interrupt me, they frustrate me, exhaust me, delight me.

My children save me.

They know I love them. They know I often think the world is terrible. And they will never stop trying to convince me otherwise. One of these days, I hope I can believe them.

EXPAND-ISTAN

Prasanta Verma

Maybe I'll imagine it this way:
not cracked or split wide open
or even scattered and broken
in a thousand pieces,
flown from the invisible hollow
of my chest into your palms,
cutting, until blood.

Maybe I'll imagine it stretched
as wide as the earth,
connected in a thousand directions,
long skinny bands, sinews,
wrapped and traveling wherever
you go, and then, it is bigger, wider, roomier
capacious, expansive enough to hold
what is poured out, and what is not given;

resilient, not easily splintered,
extended with unbreakable tendons,
generous enough for strangers and
remnants.

LIGHTING

Prasanta Verma

I light candles
on my kids' birthday cakes

I strike a match
to kindle fire in the fireplace

I roast marshmallows
on a pointed stick

I see them in the future
Laid to rest on the pyre

Log upon log
stacked, ready

They hand me the blazing torch
to ignite the death bed of fiery tradition

Is this a painless gateway to Nirvana

Is the smoke a pleasant aroma
like the incense of prayer

Will the gods bend down low, sift ashes
through god-fingers, lament, missing you

Who will collect ashes
scattered on the river

Will gods reconstruct the particles

My sins, burned to ash
He bleeds, I am whole

Where do I visit After—

rivers or gargantuan ocean

No one asked my preference—
tombstone or ashes

tell me
do I use my right hand or left

tell me
the appointed length for mourning

which began when I was told
what to do with death

STEWARD

Prasanta Verma

brush my hair with hyssop
pass me by

I   slice and   cut it
into   bite-sized pieces

for you to easily eat, grasp
with only two fingers,

appetizers on silver.
Sample, taste, see

if it is good. Others I wash, rinse,
keep warm, sheltered, safe.

I watch one grow like a tumor,
thrive and feed on me.

It ate
and was never satisfied.

I do not hoard; I am
generous, freely sharing.

I rock them to sleep,
day and night shift,

keeping vigil
over the flock.

Sometimes broken in half,
sometimes torn; I do not waste.

wash over me
blood-stained sky and earth

taste of honey
on my tongue

I divide myself   into bite-sized   poems.
I am a good steward of this pain.

SALT

Marjorie Stelmach

Stalking the base of a cinderblock wall, a lean
stub-tailed cat pours itself forward
and re-compacts, each step menace-slow and
light as a lick. I would not want to be
small prey in these fields.
                              In the middle distance,
sun shafts loll on rust-colored roofs and ruffle
the fur of the shed-boards: a scene of laudable ruin.
Some days, it feels right to be weathered.
Chipped. Un-repainted.
Surface cells scoured from the grain.
                              Of late,
I've grown, too, to favor salt over sweetness—
less indulgent, more authentic. Chemically, salt
is a pact of poisons: sodium / chlorine. We sow it
to our sorrow. But then, I savor sorrow, too:
it tastes of time.
                  It's autumn now.
Seeds of the black walnut trees lie scattered
in tough green husks on the lawn, tossed ripe
onto toxic ground at the foot
of the parent tree—where they'll rot
or be eaten.
            Only a few—
buried by squirrels, forgotten, frozen—
will earn from the deep cold the right to a future.
It's an ugly bargain:
one generation blights the earth; the next
lights out for the territories.
                              I know
I've taken safety for granted, as if it were earned.
As my life nears its end, it's sufficient to sit here
idly admiring the stalk of a molten cat—
a practiced combatant, its weapons honed
to perfection. By contrast,

                        my own kind
has mastered the strike from afar—a meld
of accuracy and denial that allows us to live
with minimal risk. When I let myself look,
I see how times change—sometimes to our sorrow:
I would not wish to be a terrorist
                                in this world.

Or a child.

VINEGAR

Marjorie Stelmach

If it's true, as they say, that our neurons can't tell
a memory of rain from a coming-down storm
or a grizzly on film from an actual beast;
if the word *ice-cream* tastes as sweet to our neurons
as real dessert, shouldn't life be a piece of cake?

> *Envision world peace.*
> *Perfect, in meditation, your tennis serve.*
> *Take both parts in the dialogue of prayer.*

But what kind of fool would settle for love's
neuronal shadow on the cranium wall,
a *postcard* of Paris, a *mirage* in the desert?
Even Jesus asked for his water drawn cold from a well,
and when, at the end, thirst raged on that hill,
a sponge of vinegar tasted, I'm sure,
exactly like vinegar.

Try it yourself: Say, you're a thief.
You've known all your life
it's a world of harm owned entirely by others.
Your death has been decreed; this day, your last.
You know all this. But still, you speak:

> *Remember me, Lord.*

Now, close your eyes and imagine Him
imagining you—I've heard worse definitions
of love—this day in His kingdom, healed, made whole.
The next thing you know, you're alive and well,
swinging axon branches in the skull
of a dying god.

Except, just now, he's a dying man,
his mind, like yours, a kingdom lit by neurons

leaping a trillion synaptic abysses
into . . . what? Paradise? Nothingness?
And yes, it's still *that* leap of faith.

SILENT NIGHT

Julie L. Moore

"USA! USA! USA!" the basketball fans, most in costumes, shout across the gym when the national anthem ends and their university's team takes the court.

Five guys dressed as Department of Transportation workers, sporting yellow helmets, orange vests, and jean shorts, raise the Stars and Stripes high above their heads as they chant. Another in their group, however, who wears a sleeveless T-shirt emblazoned with Old Glory, raises his fists.

Some students wear Spiderman's red-and-blue outfit, black-webbed polyester clinging to their bodies. Others materialize as mimes and minions, blue men and gold women, the Queen's guard and Sesame Street puppets, karate athletes and lumberjacks. Some reindeer appear, too (though not on the rooftop!), along with Santa Claus wannabes. McDonald's French Fries stand beside a cow and its accompanying chicken, mimicking mock combat, hoof to claw, a la advertising by Chick-Fil-A, which boasts a franchise in the student center. One female student even dons a bald cap and police uniform, standing with her hands to her side: doppelganger for the campus's beloved chief.

If the visiting team didn't know any better, they'd think it was Halloween, but the snow and sub-freezing temperatures as well as the game's name tell them otherwise.

Dubbed "Silent Night," this is a game that national media has covered, declaring as NBC did in 2016, the event's 20th anniversary, that it is "one of the best traditions in college sports." Students began waiting for this event outside at 1:00, so they could grab good seats—as close to the front row as possible. The hours-long goal of the annual cold line is, of course, *to be seen.*

There's nothing like it anywhere else. When all is said and done, no matter who wins (though the Athletic Director usually schedules a weak visitor), the fans all sing "Silent Night" together. But that's not the main attraction: Here, on this December night, the fans remain mute until the home team scores its tenth point. Until that time, they cheer hoops with hands upraised, each finger waggling in waves, rather than with cheering and clapping. Quiet as the cornfields surrounding this

Indiana school, participants are certainly not passive but rather premeditated and persistent in their silence.

The more hushed the crowd is, the more explosive the point.

***

In August of 2014, in a Walmart located just twenty minutes from my previous home in southwest Ohio, John Crawford III picked up a BB/pellet air rifle and walked up and down aisles while he chatted on his cell phone with his girlfriend at the time. He was breaking no Ohio law, as a professor and former police chief told me later.

I've watched the security camera's video of the event several times. To me, and many others, Crawford looked like any man looks when on the phone with a woman insisting on something: engrossed in that conversation and unaware of his surroundings. Maybe he picked up the toy gun to have something for his hands to do, like my son fiddles with salt and pepper shakers at the dinner table or my daughter peels rivulets of wax from the sides of long-lit tapers. Whatever the reason, Crawford was barely paying attention to what he was doing, but he wasn't aiming the gun at anyone or anything. Yet, the 9-1-1 caller told the operator Crawford was "pointing it at people."

The video also shows how officers didn't hesitate for a moment. They interpreted the caller's statement as an active shooter situation. So within a second of seeing him, they downed Crawford, whom doctors pronounced dead at the hospital.

That had happened near an upscale mall and expensive restaurants and elite coffee roasters, all places I'd frequented when I lived for decades in Ohio. It felt like it happened in my own backyard.

***

"[T]he essence of a double bind is two conflicting demands, each on a different logical level, neither of which can be ignored or escaped. This leaves the subject torn both ways, so that whichever demand they try to meet, the other demand cannot be met. 'I must do it, but I can't do it' is a typical description of the double-bind experience," posited Gregory Bateson, the anthropologist who coined the term.

Double binds often occur in abusive relationships, with abusers creating the impossible logic. Sometimes, however, the double bind occurs when two seemingly compatible statements come in conflict, tearing them asunder and forcing a choice, as if one can be made without consequence.

To wit:

Love your country. Sing her praises. Be grateful for the freedoms you have. Pledge your allegiance.

Love your fellow humans. Fight injustice which harms them. Fight for their freedom. Give voice to those who have no voice.

***

Leading up to the 21st event, excitement built on campus and for the first time ever, everyone who wanted to attend the famous game had to secure a ticket. Fire codes and public safety being what they are, the school finally decided that for the collective good, they had to limit attendance.

As a faculty member, therefore, I had to enter a lottery to acquire a seat. New this year, thanks to my move from Ohio, I had seen media coverage about the event before and was hearing all the hype from students, so I decided to throw my hat into that digital ring.

With whom would I go? Most of my colleagues had *been there, done that*, so I contacted a friend about whether she might be going. And indeed, she was. But, she said, it was complicated.

***

Several months ago, in the New York heat of an August afternoon, Frank Serpico, now 81, gave a speech. Serpico is famous for blowing the whistle on corruption in the NYPD half a century ago (and whose story inspired the Al Pacino movie), although young people may not know who he is now.

Eighty fellow police officers surrounded Serpico as they stood together before the Brooklyn Bridge. According to *The New York Times*, Serpico said he was there "to support anyone who has the courage to stand up against injustice and oppression anywhere in this country and the world."

"Anyone," in this context, specifically referred to Colin Kaepernick.

Edwin Raymond, a sergeant in the NYPD presently, organized the event and spoke as well: "As members of law enforcement, we can confirm that the issues [Kaepernick] is saying exist in policing, and throughout the criminal justice system, indeed exist."

***

Thanks to the old spiritual, children learn early on that the "knee bone's connected to the thigh bone." This is no mystery, even to the toddler, as she touches her ankle, then shin bone in sync, and moves to her knee (on which, in a different tune, she might play knick-knack and sing the refrain, "This old man came rolling home!").

Often, however, the context of the song *is* a mystery, leaving children and adults alike ignorant about the fact that this is the Valley of Dry Bones we're talking about. This is Ezekiel's terrifying vision of Israelis' flesh husked from their skeletons, their exile vividly illustrated. *Sh'ma Yisrael Adonai Eloheinu Adonai Echad,* Jehovah had instructed them. But they had ceased to hear; they had mistreated the poor and raised idols above the Lord they tired of. They were, therefore, stuck in Babylon.

In this valley vision, God asked the prophet, "Son of man, can these bones live?"

Ezekiel knew God knew the answer—and said so—but sometimes, I wonder if between the lines, the all-too-human prophet wondered, "Why in the world are you asking *me*?!"

God is forthright thereafter. He promises Ezekiel He will dress the bones in tissues and tendons, flesh and hair; He will resurrect them. He promises Ezekiel, "They will no longer defile themselves with their idols and vile images or with any of their offenses, for I will save them."

Of course, Ezekiel had no idea when all this would happen. But he heard the word of the Lord and obeyed: He preached the prophecies, hoping in the one and only true God.

So the knee bone suddenly seems more important than a jingle or a lesson about our skeletal structures. The fact that James Weldon Johnson wrote the song makes it equally important for Americans. What was the early leader of the NAACP, who fought for federal laws against lynching, and a poet in the Harlem Renaissance doing writing a children's song?

Answer: Nothing. This was no such ditty. This was no knick-knack on a drum or shoe.

These lyrics promised African-Americans that their bones would rise again, that though they, too, were exiled from their homeland, through no fault of their own, they would see Jehovah restore them. The performers' voices ran up and down the spinal cord connecting head to toe, horrifying past to painful present, and present to glorious future.

So what could it mean more than a century later that an African-American adopted into a white family—and adopted as a son of God according to his own outspoken testimony—bends his knee bone before a flag raised above him prior to a football game, praying for justice for his brothers and sisters, seeking resurrection of the all-too-many dry bones that have littered American streets?

The bones of boys like Tamir Rice, the 12-year-old with an airsoft gun, the boy the 9-1-1 caller clearly identified as a "juvenile." Shot by police who violated many a protocol when they pulled their cruiser up to him just a month before Christmas, Tamir fell, his single wound a crimson ribbon unraveling in the snow. Can you hear Tamir's mom keening with the Hebrew mothers in "The Coventry Carol" for the sons cut down by Herod's knife?

That woe is me, poor child, for thee
And ever mourn and may
For thy parting neither say nor sing
Bye, bye, lully, lullay.

There are so many more bones.

Bones of women like 92-year-old Kathryn Johnson, shot 39 times by Atlanta police, and Alberta Spruill, a city employee readying for work in New York City, both killed in "no-knock" drug raids based upon false information.

Bones of men like John Crawford III.

The bones of Eric Garner. Face shoved into cement with four officers restraining him, Garner, apparently guilty of selling individual, untaxed cigarettes—"loosies"—repeated not once or twice or even thrice, but eleven different times, "I can't breathe." And the coroner ruled that Officer Daniel Pantaleo's illegal choke hold constituted homicide.

"Prophesy to the breath," Adonai told Ezekiel. "Prophesy, son of man, and say to it, 'This is what the Sovereign LORD says: Come from the four winds, O breath, and breathe into these slain, that they may live.'"

***

My daughter once suffered a dislocated knee cap. It is a gruesome injury, but it happened quickly. Playing basketball at a summer camp, a fellow athlete knocked into her knee and shoved her patella aside. For others, changing direction while simultaneously planting one's foot can cause the dislocation.

Either way, one thing's for sure: The knee cap endures tremendous stress it cannot resist.

My daughter required surgery to repair it and her overstretched medial collateral ligament. The pediatric orthopedic surgeon came highly recommended and ably made the repair.

A few years later, he was arrested and convicted of raping a 16-year-old girl. Three times. We could have defended him, truthfully asserting he never touched my daughter, so he should be left alone, he should be respected, and he should keep his job. He's a brilliant surgeon.

But we didn't for obvious reasons: Evil isn't evil all the time. People who commit crimes can, in other spheres, do good. Like the rest of us, each criminal's character has multiple dimensions. One may hate his neighbor but love his mother; another may perform magnificent surgeries but mar a young lady. And one is all it takes. Although Andre Agassi used to declare as he lowered his black sunglasses in the old Canon camera ad, *Image is everything*, we know better. It's easier to manage appearances than reality; it's easier to look good, even in some cases, do good, than to actually *be* good.

***

My friend and I enter the gym, meeting another friend and fifty students where they chose to sit: on the visitors' bleachers—the section closest to the door—because it is not inaccurate to say we want to be seen as well, albeit for different reasons. Nor is it inaccurate to say being close to the door brings a certain degree of comfort: a quick exit is possible, if necessary. African-Americans, Hispanic-Americans, Asian-Americans, international students, and a handful of whites like me hug and encourage each other. Dressed in black, we wear no humorous attire, unless, for some reason, you count the few in Kaepernick T-shirts, his afro doubling for a fist.

Most of us are nervous, but some are frightened. Some white students communicated threats earlier in the week, announcing they had friends who'd "kick anyone's ass" who "took a knee." So some administrators are nervous, too, having called meetings all week to make sure everything would be *okay*. The main theme went something like this: *Media will be there. You have to realize there are ramifications for every action.* In one meeting with students, however, they actually didn't speak, hoping activist students and two African-American staff members, my friends, would bear the white man's burden they seemed uncomfortable carrying.

Here I am, brand new to the school, assembled with this group of hurting students. I wonder at one point what I'm doing and how the last thing I want to do is bite the hand that now feeds me. After all, I understand complicated ties to donors and constituency, to a stable reputation, to quiet faith and a concern for students' safety bind the school's leaders to a certain extent.

I also know I am disgracing some in my own family who vehemently oppose Kaepernick and believe him to be disrespectful and ungrateful. I feel their shame on my shoulders.

Before the tip-off, pop music blares as the costume-clad students gather, laugh, and converse. The blue men's spray-painted caps require adjustments and even, in one case, removal, so one kid can scratch his head with gusto. Cheerleaders in Mrs. Claus get-ups prance around the court; several shirtless guys in black shorts form a horizontal line in the front row of the home section, diagonally across from us, then lift signs that altogether spell, *Censored*.

There is no pep band and no drunkenness. The campus is dry and the students sober. Some professors and staff members show up with their families and walk past us on their way to concessions and back—with red-striped boxes of popcorn and Pepsi in hand.

Celebration—and safe, clean fun—actually seem the theme of the evening.

Eventually, a student-generated music video airs over the jumbotron: The diverse rappers—black and white, male and female—seem to embody hip hop, but most students in the video jive to music whose roots delve beneath impoverished, dangerous, underprivileged paths they've never walked. It is what it is in east central Indiana. Seeing diverse students singing together, truly having fun, has merit that can transcend mere entertainment.

Still, though, I cannot not quite discern the lyrics above the noise, except for the repetition of the words, "silent night." The hip-hop beat, not the words, drives the gyrations on screen and in the house. And having taught for ten years at Wilberforce University, our nation's oldest liberal arts HBCU, in the 1990s, I learned a thing or two about Dr. Dre and N.W.A. (one student once warned me, "You can't listen to that, Ms. Moore; it's too much for you. Seriously"), Snoop Dogg and LL Cool J, 2 Pac and The Notorious B.I.G.—in short, rap (and gangsta rap) music and the then-burgeoning genre of hip hop. I know, too, the singers' hand gestures speak a language of their own, gestures some of my WU students were more than willing to demonstrate:

The Mos-Def Wave
Back-Up-Off-Me Hands
World Hands
The Slim Shady Chop
Not-Having-It Hands

Each one conjures their eponymous images ubiquitous in the music. I see these gestures in the students' video, hands and fingers waving, bending, and flexing.

They strike me as somehow anachronistic, not because of the problem of time but because of the problem of origin.

These gestures aren't merely meant to generate MC swag. Indeed, emcees and rappers alike attempt to tap into what KRS-One refers to as "collective consciousness," which really is another way of answering the same question I ask my students to consider when they write their essays: Who is your audience and what are they thinking about? In urban areas, that's poverty. That's a lack of affordable homes, safe neighborhoods, and self-supporting work. That's paying more for food than your suburban counterparts. That's cruel or unfair landlords or employers. That's police brutality.

Hip Hop has always been political.

It emanates from Malcolm X's desire to end the oppression and exploitation of the African diaspora. It comes from Martin Luther King, Jr.'s dream for equality. His vision wasn't located in a valley of despair but on a mountaintop of economic empowerment.

When the situation in Ferguson exploded as Michael Brown's body lay slain and bloody—for hours—on that Missouri pavement, the protests and grief that overwhelmed not only the city but also the nation were nothing new. As Mamie Elizabeth Till-Mobley could tell you, if she were still alive, Blacks have suffered under racism's myriad cruelties since the nation's beginning, though its shapes constantly shift. It changes costumes every few decades.

More recently, rappers started chronicling such brutality in the 1970s when Afrika Bambaataa, an immigrant of Jamaican and Barbadian lineage, founded the Universal Zulu Nation through which developed the subculture and art movement now known as hip hop. Bambaataa defined the four main pillars of hip hop music: rapping; using record players like instruments, to create music in the form of beats, scratches, etc.; breakdancing; and creating graffiti art. Since hip hop is considered more of a culture than a genre of music, however, other elements follow closely behind, including a thorough knowledge of the history, philosophy, language, and intellectualism associated with the movement.

No wonder KRS-One points out this vital truth: "Rap is something that is done. Hip Hop is something that is lived." No wonder Kendrick Lamar, like Flannery O'Connor before him, penetrates reality, no matter how ugly or profane, for all of it he's witnessed during a Compton childhood—"murder, conviction, / Burners, boosters, burglars, ballers, dead, redemption / Scholars, fathers dead with kids." Lamar also raps in that same song, appropriately titled "DNA," "My expertise checked out in second grade / When I was 9, on cell, motel, we didn't have nowhere to stay." This is the childhood that leaves him with nothing but longing: "I wish I was fed forgiveness."

Which brings us back to those hands. Rappers look as though they are conducting the music, the symphony of the streets. And they interpret their stories, which they have lived—and which some of their friends and families *don't* live through.

During the video at the game, I begin to wonder how many American-born-and-bred fans dancing in this gym, in this rural, Indiana town, have *lived* hip hop? And what is our safe, suburban DNA composed of? Can we who have never known *want*—in the biblical or even Dickensian sense—who have asked time and again for someone, anyone, to hide it beneath his cloak so as not to dwell too much on negativity, on ugliness, on impossibility—for the poor we will have always, as the Good Shepherd even said—use these gestures nearly unconsciously, as if just for show?

Poet Adrienne Rich once said, "Art means nothing if it simply decorates the dinner table of the power which holds it hostage."

Maybe there's room for sympathy, though. Maybe those who enjoy the privilege of a comfortable neighborhood, a college education, and the confidence of belief are caught in a double bind, too?

Be yourself. Have fun. You're only young once. Pursue happiness. Attain the American dream.

Be a servant. Humble yourself before the Lord. Esteem others over self, Kingdom over country.

***

It's terrible. It's so disrespectful. He's so ungrateful for what he has, for what veterans have lost their lives for. He's rich, for Pete's sakes. What does he have to complain about?

Kaepernick started out by sitting during the anthem, yet, after a fellow football player, Army Special Forces veteran Nate Boyer, shared his perspectives on the protest, the players together decided Kaepernick should kneel instead of sit.

Boyer himself has said, "Soldiers take a knee in front of a fallen brother's grave, you know, to show respect." He told Kaepernick that "taking a knee would be a little more respectful [than sitting]. It's still a demonstration. You're still saying something but, people take a knee to pray."

What is the point of free speech if veterans' deaths negate it? Do those in the military fight only for the appearance of freedom but not its actuality, a symbol without a spine?

God forbid.

As Eric Reid explains in his Op-Ed for *The New York Times,* "We chose to kneel because it's a respectful gesture. I remember thinking our posture was like a flag flown at half-mast to mark a tragedy."

What tragedy?

"There is police brutality. People of color have been targeted by police," Kaepernick says, making his reasons for his demonstration clear. "So that's something that this country has to change. There's things we can do to hold them more accountable. Make those standards higher. You have people that practice law and are lawyers and go to school for eight years, but you can become a cop in six months and don't have to have the same amount of training as a cosmetologist. That's insane. Someone that's holding a curling iron has more education and more training that [sic] people that have a gun and are going out on the street to protect us."

A curling iron? Seriously? That's just silly. Besides, those guys were all breaking the law. And it's 7 years for a lawyer. Get your facts straight, man.

"Thou shalt love the Lord thy God with all thy heart, and with all thy soul, and with all thy mind. This is the first and great commandment. And the second is like unto it, Thou shalt love thy neighbor as thyself. On these two commandments hang all the law and the prophets."

"But I tell you, do not resist an evil person. If anyone slaps you on the right cheek, turn to them the other cheek also. If it is possible, as far as it depends on you, live at peace with everyone."

They should choose another way to demonstrate.

Kaepernick and Reid are both professing Christians who attribute their activism to their faith. In fact, Reid has said James 2:17 compelled him to action, saying he had to wed works to his faith. Doing so was obedience to his Lord.

Reid says the killing of Alton Sterling in Reid's own backyard, Baton Rouge, Louisiana, gave birth to his activism. Two officers shot Sterling multiple times in the chest at close range. Suddenly, the police killings that had disturbed Reid grew intensely personal; he realized anything like that could've happened to his own family members in his hometown. Anything like that could still happen.

So he joined Kaepernick in kneeling.

But the Bible says to submit to our government. Besides, they're paid to play, not to get political.

I fear not the John Crawfords of this world but the system that misjudged the deer in headlights for a lion on the prowl. And the culture that is happy with Blacks as long as they produce what it wants to use. The same culture that produced Dylann Roof, who, one year after the Crawford killing, walked into a prayer meeting and slaughtered nine Black Christians who'd welcomed him in peace. *Bye, bye, Lully, Lullay.*

***

The U.S. Flag Code states that everyone present during the performance of the national anthem should "stand at attention facing the flag with the right hand over the heart." In addition, men should remove their hats, unless they're in uniform.

Interestingly, according to the U.S. Flag Code, "The flag represents a living country and *is itself considered a living thing*" (emphasis mine). This is why anyone wearing a flag pin must affix it on his left lapel, for that is the one nearest the heart.

As a living thing, the flag commands respect, so the code also says, "The flag should never be used as wearing apparel, bedding, or drapery. It should never be festooned, drawn back, nor up, in folds, but always allowed to fall free."

Likewise, the code says the flag should "never touch anything beneath it, such as the ground, the floor, water, or merchandise" nor should it "ever be used as a costume or athletic uniform." Furthermore, one should never carry the flag "flat or horizontally" but should bear it strategically so it is always "aloft and free."

Finally, when a flag becomes so worn out that it is no longer fit to fly, the owner should, according to the code, dispose of the flag in a dignified ceremony. Simply throwing the flag into the trash violates the code as would burying it. Instead, one should fold the flag neatly and burn it. Although in Indiana, burning a flag can result in a misdemeanor charge, the law makes this exception so owners can burn it in a bonfire pit as they pledge their allegiance and bid adieu.

***

Eventually, the university choir director leads the choir out to the court. The music stirs.

Before we arrive at that point, however, we need deliverance from the DoT guys, including the one festooned with flag. These road-worker imitators seem committed to standing in front of us, forming as they do, a kind of offensive screen. And their line has movement, as they take one, then two steps back, pushing into us.

The student with the flag abruptly raises it shoulder-high, sparing it from his sweat for a moment. Then he crumples it in his hands like an empty burlap sack not yet ready to contain anything.

The police chief approaches, speaks softly, takes one guy by the arm, gently, then leads them all across the court. They stop in the home section, directly across from us, and seem quite pleased with their new placement. One wraps his flag around his shoulders again, but unevenly now, as the bottom red corner grazes the floor like a speck of blood.

We lack comfort on our side. The song plays. Our bodies become our flags, at half-mast.

I do not put my hand over my heart. I do not adore the elaborate, symbolic fabric. I put my head in my hand, pray to the only living one who can save us. I ask God for unity, for harmony, pleading that He redeem students who've voiced racial epithets without remorse and scrawled slurs on bathroom stalls, begging for peace for the students who suffered the insults. I ask forgiveness for my own failures and faults.

I pray for love above all else, because God is love, because we know hatred is borne of idolatry, and we know an idol when we see one. (Idols are not inanimate objects. They are living things. And when anyone faces losing them, he holds on tighter, and they hold on, too. Their name is legion.)

And after, as we rise, the still-helmeted road workers lead that unmistakable cheer from the other side—the deafening answer to our prayers, for *no* is an answer, too—that chant begun when the U.S. hockey team miraculously conquered the Soviets in 1980.

Three letters, shouted over and over again. Vowel, consonant, vowel.

The Stars and Stripes rise, too, and the cheer unites patriotic instincts with something else, something animalistic, even, but something I can't quite name.

Whatever it is, it brings back that ice, that red stare, that Siberian punishment for loss.

***

In December 2014, after both the incidents with Tamir Rice and John Crawford III (and a year or so after the Black Lives Matter movement began), Ohio's Attorney General Mike DeWine set up the Advisory Group on Law Enforcement Training, which recommended twenty-five specific changes in police training. In so doing, Ohio leads the way in analyzing not only that training but also officers' relationships with the community.

Whereas before the incidents, according to the *Akron-Beacon Journal*, in Ohio, "police academy candidates only needed to be over 18 years old and eligible to carry a gun," now candidates must possess "a high school diploma or GED," pass drug tests, and undergo fitness evaluations. Moreover, the academy now teaches officers how to address their "inherent biases," communicate to and behave appropriately with the mentally ill, and develop meaningful relationships with their community members. Finally, training now requires candidates to practice approved approaches in specific and high-stress situations.

In a statement eerily close to Serpico's, Akron Police Chief James Nice said, "When you look at some of these bad situations, where the police officer was wrong, sometimes you find out that person should never have been an officer."

Ah, so Black lives do matter.

Indeed, what American has never, not once, criticized her country about anything? Who has never argued for solutions to national or local problems, at least over dinner conversations? Who actually disagrees with Reid when he makes this most American of statements: "It has always been my understanding that the brave men and women who fought and died for our country did so to ensure that we could live in a fair and free society, which includes the right to speak out in protest. It should go without saying that I love my country and I'm proud to be an American. But, to quote James Baldwin, 'exactly for this reason, I insist on the right to criticize her perpetually'"?

Knee bone connected to the thigh bone
Thigh bone connected to the hip bone
Hip bone connected to the back bone

***

Every American knows the first verse of "The Star-Spangled Banner" by heart, singing it as we often do at sports games, the most popular venue where it's played. (Why sports games, amateur and professional, have become married to the anthem is a bit of a mystery to me.) Most Americans also know Francis Scott Key wrote the anthem amid the War of 1812 and wrote several other verses, too, though they may not know what they say. They know, too, that Key wrote it after seeing not the red cross of the Union Jack but the red stripes of Old Glory herself rising in victory over Fort McHenry following a British barrage of bombing on Baltimore—25 hours' worth, in fact. And of course, they believe the U.S. won the war, even though our beloved neighbors to the north will tell us otherwise when we travel to Canada.

Some Americans may erroneously believe Key was imprisoned upon a British ship during the attack on Baltimore, but that wasn't the case. Although impressment—the practice the Brits had of forcing American seamen off their ships to fight for the King—was one reason for the war, Key was not, forgive the pun, in that sort of boat. Instead, he was there on official business, lawyer that he was, negotiating—successfully, as it turned out—the release of an American prisoner with a fellow lawyer who accompanied him. The British insisted only that they complete their attack before the three Americans disembark. Sure, Key was ecstatic to see those stripes waving the next day, but he was free to go either way.

Very few Americans know that Key was, like most of his aristocratic counterparts of his day, unopposed to slavery. In fact, he grew up on a Maryland plantation that owned nearly 200 slaves, and Key believed all Blacks to be "a distinct and inferior race of people, which all experience proves to be the greatest evil that afflicts a community."

Just as bad, in his legal career, Key made a name for himself by trying to infringe on abolitionists' free speech. *The Smithsonian* reports that in the case *U.S. v. Reuben Crandall*, "Key made national headlines by asking whether the property rights of slaveholders outweighed the free speech rights of those arguing for slavery's abolishment. Key hoped to silence abolitionists, who, he charged, wished to 'associate and amalgamate with the negro.'"

Americans could argue that this tawdry side to our national anthem's author merely puts him in the same camp as most of our founding fathers (except the Quakers), and thus, that Key was just a man of his time. They could likewise truthfully point out that Key did represent Black clients during his legal career, something he didn't have to do but did. Both arguments have some merit.

But could those Americans likewise argue Key's racist views about Blacks and slavery are therefore irrelevant to the anthem we stand for, sing to, and laud with patriotic passion? Could they convince us that if Key had won his case, successfully prosecuting the abolitionist Reuben Crandall for publishing his pamphlets and fliers, that we'd still have the right to free speech?

One could try. But certainly, Key didn't have African-Americans in mind as being either free or brave. And the anthem's third verse is a killer.

Many historians believe that alludes to the Battle of Bladensburg, which took place just two weeks before the bombardment on Fort

McHenry and which historian Daniel Walker Howe, calls "the greatest disgrace ever dealt to American arms." At that battle, the Brits socked it to us, with the help of the Corps of Colonial Marines, composed entirely of American refugee slaves. Admiral Alexander Cochrane of the Royal Navy had issued a proclamation, liberating any slaves willing to fight the Americans. Thousands of enslaved families made their way to the Brits' ships on the Chesapeake. Six hundred join that Corps.

Although the American forces initially banned slaves from their regiments, eventually, after some major losses (including the failure to expand into Canada), they desperately needed more men, so some slaves did join their forces. But for those who fought for the British, their motivation is easy enough to understand. After all, why would slaves feel patriotic about or grateful for the country that had so enslaved them? What did they have to lose? And why wouldn't they fight for the refuge offered them, indeed, for their freedom, the same thing the Americans said they were fighting for?

And then there's this: Imagine the terror of slave owners who may have to face their former slaves in battle; the psychological toll was torturous, and Cochrane, knighted in the end, knew it. Yet, when the Americans defeated the Royal Navy in Baltimore, imagine, too, the sense of vindication those same slave owners might have felt. The euphoria over defeating not only the King but also their rebellious slaves.

And then read, or sing, if you dare, our anthem's third verse:

> And where is that band who so vauntingly swore,
> That the havoc of war and the battle's confusion
> A home and a Country should leave us no more?
> Their blood has wash'd out their foul footstep's pollution.
> No refuge could save the hireling and slave
> From the terror of flight or the gloom of the grave,
> And the star-spangled banner in triumph doth wave
> O'er the land of the free and the home of the brave.

Then see this: The two white police officers, fully clad in uniform, atop Alton Sterling, who lies on his back on the concrete. One man's knee leans in to Sterling's gut, while the other officer's knee traps his arm. Guns out of holsters, in their hands, pressing against Sterling's black chest. Words fly: I swear to God.

Oh, the havoc of war, the battle's confusion. What foul footsteps can his blood ever wash out?

***

The local news reports about the game are typical of the past 21 years: The students were silent (how cool), the tenth point scored (so cool), and the place exploded with students storming the court and cheering as if their lives depended on it (coolest tradition *ever*). And when the last buzzer sounded, the crowd sang "Silent Night" together.

I admit it: The tradition is cool, it really is. And amazing to experience first-hand. The rafters rattle and floor boards shake from the noise. The solemnity at the end is a juxtaposition of literary—or is it biblical?—proportions. One might even want to express with passion, in Whitman's full-throttle voice, "Oh me! Oh life!"

The announcer tells students before the game begins, "Students are not allowed to come onto the court and should stay in their seats," but they never obey. They rush in like rain, drenching everyone in their euphoria.

All too soon, though, I bemoan with Whitman the "endless trains of the faithless, of cities fill'd with the foolish." I remember that I am the most faithless and foolish of all, returning as I do, afterwards, to warm home and loving dog. I can walk around my new hometown—a sundown town into the 1990s, no less—any day of the week white and thus, unassailed by suspicion or the burden of representing my race every time I speak.

My friend thanks me for "standing in the gap" with her, but I tell her not to because it cost her a helluva lot—students had organized and led it, but she bore the brunt of accusations and suspicions and grief. It costs me nothing. I blend in to the woodwork.

In dismay, I bow my head again, wondering whether there will ever be peace on earth. Because the local media says nothing about the demonstration. Because the university waves its *not-having-it hands* so the highlight reel shows nothing but fans crazed by excitement, glory garnered from the victory, and tradition extended and extending for as long as anyone can see.

How cool can any event be when the real news is an erasure no one recognizes?

If students risk ass and attitude but are not seen, did their kneeling even happen?

I would like to believe, as Whitman did, the answer is that they were there, "that life exists and identity, / That the powerful play goes on, and [they] may contribute a verse."

I want to preach that longed-for truth from mountain tops and flat Indiana plains alike.

But those students are in a bind, and though they hope *dem bones gonna rise again,* they've grown weary and worn as the country they want to love uses its name against them.

They can't quite see how that play ends.

***

Epilogue, of sorts:

PR erasure notwithstanding, in the month following the protest, the university began to develop a new system through which students can now file complaints about racial slurs and racist behaviors. Title IX, of course, does not cover such incidents. The Office of Intercultural Programs also hosted a panel of five people—three students, one OIP staff member, and myself—who had taken a knee at the game. Eighty-five students and some other deans and faculty attended. Interaction was civil. We shared our perspectives, and my fellow panelists spoke to the racist behavior they'd encountered—and their friends and family had experienced—back at home, in the area, or on campus. One student, who's from the south side of Chicago, related his own terrifying experience of a mistaken "no knock" raid on his family's house. They all survived, but not without deep scars and an even deeper distrust of the police. Although a couple of questions from the audience seemed to evidence a lack of awareness, we addressed them as respectfully as possible. Most attendees asked sensitive, thoughtful questions, and discussion could've continued for a long time. We know many are wrestling with perspectives different from their own and struggling to understand how something that once was so obvious and unquestionable to them—allegiance to the flag—has never been either for many other Americans. It was January, and temperatures outside hovered around zero. Yet, a thaw may have begun that evening—may have begun when students' knees fell to that gymnasium floor. We know the recurring freezes that can go with that "may," however; we know what an arctic blast can do. Prayer and perseverance are the real names of this game.

LAKESIDE, WITH JONATHAN

Jeannie Prinsen

To the waterfront at Lake Ontario Park we go,
you leading the way to your favourite place: down,

down stone steps to the little cobble beach, where a shelf
of flat rocks stretches into the water. Cross-legged

on a rock, you gaze at the lake, its wind-ruffled surface
dancing with a million bright diamonds. You call out

to the gulls that wheel across the sky, and watch
a half-dozen geese skim the water then swoop

swiftly up and away. You look around
with a smile and say *Happy.*

This is as abstract as you get, you whose mind anchors
firmly in the tangibles: supper, school, garbage truck.

No bedtime confidences for you, no heartfelt talks
of dreams or hopes, just the familiar, daily repetition.

I could choose to grieve what's not, or let you teach me
that peace abides in the way water swells and breaks

again and again on the shore, that the seabirds speak
to you as they cry overhead, that the windmills

over on the island are your friends, tall and steady
in the sunlight, their long arms waving hello.

ON NEEDING SOMEONE TO BE A LITTLE LIKE GOD

Kimberly Ann Priest

My son falls into the arms
of an overstuffed chair
and imitates his father
watching TV,
remote in hand, seduced
until he hears
the knob turn
on the trailer's backdoor
and lurches forward,
out of the chair,
bounding toward
the groan and clack
of hinges and feet,
trembling with facts
learned from cartoons
and fingers flavored
with crackers and cheese,
charging into
his father's open arms,
half a reflection of me
standing in the kitchen
with paring knife in hand,
seduced—
needing someone to be
a little like God
feeding, clothing, listening
as we try to understand
His absence from our day.

CONSIDER THE LOQUAT

Kimberly Ann Priest

written after leaving my daughter to start
a new life after divorce

I pack your liver into my suitcase
since I would not feel generous or poetic
stealing away your heart

and since liver means the same as heart
in ancient poetry,
and I imagine this is because

like them I feel this pain
in my gut, not my chest, as though
the wind has been knocked out of me

so hard I'm not sure I am doing
the thing I am doing—
leaving you.

I'm not sure I can see it this way,
not now; rather,
I must pretend that we are doing something

different. Perhaps, going on extended
separate journeys. Or, submitting ourselves
to some divinely ordained plan.

Maybe we are a river
breaking in its path to form two independent
streams,

or we are like the loquat that blooms
out of season
and I should not think about this whole thing

too much, about
how it might be unnatural to leave you
at fifteen, barely a woman,

assuring me that now is a good time
to go—as though the deep reds
and yellows of autumn are a sign,

a portent,
and I would be a fool if I did not heed
the warning in your eyes. You know me

too well, my daughter. You know
I will feel this pain long enough to wish
I had stolen your heart.

THE RIVER

Andrew Koenig

A blank sky the color of old sink water. Wind brushing along the snowy ground and through the trees, mere skeletons. The river was a vein slicing through the snow like the lines under his papery skin. He could see it through the living room window, watch it churn and glide through the fall, then die in the winter. What happened to the fish? Were they frozen through? Was there enough space beneath the ice for them to swim? Did they recycle dirty air until they suffocated? He pressed his small face against the glass, opaqued by his breath, and cataloged these questions for his parents and teachers. They had an answer for everything.

He had a sister who went to the river once. An adventure for big kids only, and he is small. He ran to their room and cried at her rejection, wondering if this meant she didn't love him anymore.

She left, and she has not returned.

Then there was a fence between the house and the river, like a fresh scar cutting against the blank snow. His parents cried and fought. There was a party that wasn't for him, but people brought him gifts. Little tokens to preserve his innocence. He was excited to share them—a miniature basketball hoop, a new set of Legos—but his parents did not seem interested, and his sister was gone. It must have been some adventure.

First there was peace. No echoes of footsteps following, no compromises to be made over what to watch on TV or the rules of his imagined kingdoms. But the peace soon became only silence, then emptiness. There were no more games, no more funny faces or laughter in the dark after their mother put them to bed. His young life had been filled with company and camaraderie, never a moment spent alone. Now he turns inward in these moments he should have been spending with his sister, telling himself stories about spaceships and superheroes. He knew that the river would return her any day and he could hear all about the adventure. Did she make it all the way to the ocean? Pirates? Mermaids with flaxen hair resting on the shoals? All things from movies, which taught him that everyone always comes home.

His mother puts him to bed and asks him to pray. He thanks God for school, for his friends and his toys. When he gets stuck, his mother reminds him to be thankful for his food and the roof over his head. He echoes this, feeling foolish at having forgotten.

He asks God to keep his sister safe on her trip. He wonders aloud if she will come home soon, and if she will bring him and his parents treasures from the sea. He prays that she will not find another brother, that she will remember him while she is gone. He finishes with an amen. His mother tucks him in tightly and leaves in heavy silence.

***

Winter passes, not slowly, but all at once, as if the blanket of snow had been torn from the ground overnight. The sun hangs in the air, exposing the backyard—a graveyard for cheap plastic beach toys and bits of trash. He scampers along the fenceline, flinging muck into a bucket, picking out pill bugs with shaking fingers. Sometimes, he stands and shouts into the river, asking where his sister has gone and if she would ever come back.

Loss is never finalized; it does not have a capacity or exist in totality. Even when something is removed, memories and habits are forever tainted with bitterness. He does not understand this yet—if his sister is gone, then everything about her must be gone as well. Her disappearance has threatened to steal away every day up to now. When he calls downstream and hears no response, the vacuum tears a little wider.

He finds strands of hair in the bathroom, as if carried up the river and through the pipes and spat into the sink. They are the same color as his sister's; he saves them in a jar, a gift for when she returns. When the jar is full, he empties the hair into a shopping bag which he fills with other things of hers he's found—a Looney Tunes t-shirt, some hair ribbons and nail polish. With markers he draws a face with a wide smile and blue, unblinking eyes. It would have to do for now.

He loves this new sister. He carries her around with him, from room to room and into the yard. He shows her the bugs he's collected, the empty corner of the yard where the new swingset will go. He points to the fence, tells her how he misses playing by the river. At dinner, he feeds her, smearing spaghetti sauce across her face and laughing. They go to bed and he whispers to her under the covers—secrets about their parents fighting, stories about the lady with spiked grey hair he has met with at school who asks about her. He kisses her, tasting the bitter residue of the marker.

In the silence before sleeping, he thinks of the days ahead with delight, and he wakes with vigor. He cannot wait to get to school, to show his sister to his friends and take her down the slide at recess. He clutches her tightly to his chest as his mother walks him to the door. He sits in his seat and shows his sister his desk while his mother talks to his teacher, whispering and glancing in his direction every few seconds.

The other kids stare. They do not know what to make of this surrogate, this bag of trash and hair. He tries to play with them, sister in tow, but they laugh. He is hurt, but he tells his sister that it's okay, sometimes kids can be mean when they're just trying to be your friend.

They head to the playground; out of range of supervision, the taunting intensifies. They call him names, push him lightly, try to steal his sister. He does not understand what he has done to deserve this; being oneself has never been a grounds for punishment.

At last, one of the bigger boys snatches the bag from his grip and flees. He gives chase, but he is too slow. The bully circles back and others surround him, tossing his sister back and forth. She arcs slightly out of his reaching hands. He tries to be strong, wants more than anything to be bigger and older. He begins to cry.

The bell rings; he is rescued from torment. The bullies break their circle and all but one sprint back to their classrooms. The last one rips the bag in two and sneers in his face, hissing the things he has heard his parents say but has never fully understood. In crisis, the truth becomes obvious, paralyzing.

She is not coming back from the river. She is a ghost haunting his house. She is dead, forever.

***

The summer's heat lurks around the house like a stray dog, its presence suffocating between the walls. Rain falls and fills the river, pushing the waters past its banks. The grass in the yard has sprung to life, prickly brown replaced with a lush green carpet. His parents say he should be playing outside, but he is too afraid.

He made another sister, but he couldn't get the face quite right, so he did not love it as much. The bag has torn, the magic marker smile has faded. He does not want to play with it, much less look at it, so he hides it under some dirty clothes. No matter how hard he tries to get away from it, his parents keep dragging it back out, thinking it will continue to offer comfort though it only amplifies the loneliness. This was never his sister. She was never here.

He no longer wants to eat. Sometimes he cries, provoked by the slightest thought of her. His parents moved her furniture out of his room, and now he cannot sleep. It is too empty; the smallest sound echoes, frightening him. These days are lost; they carry no meaning, no joy. He still feels her.

But if he still feels her, she cannot be gone forever. She is alive in the spirit of his days, so it cannot be too much to think that she is also alive somewhere else. From the living room, he watches the river. It barely flows. It can be tamed.

He puts on his swimming goggles and trunks and slips out the back door, then scales the fence. It has been so long since he has been here, on the other side. It feels like virgin land, and he feels like an intruder. Groundwater seeps between his toes and he wonders if he is brave enough to do this. He can hold his breath, and he can kick and paddle (though not in tandem), but what will he do once he steps in? In which direction did her adventure take her? If he chooses incorrectly, he too might be lost to the river.

But his intuition tells him to press on, to wade in. It is colder than anything that gives life ought to be. He shivers and again thinks of turning back, but he is urged on by everything that has failed in this season—unfulfilled wishes made on birthday candles and bedtime prayers unheard. If she won't come back and if nothing else will bring her home, then he will find her himself.

The water flows around him slowly, right to left. He takes a big gulp of air, pinches his nose, and drops. To submerge is no small task; he has only done it a handful of times. He is proud.

He sits for a moment, suspended in the rushing waters that push him along slowly. He opens his eyes: everything around him is the color of vomit, and it is all he sees. With one hand on his nose, he orients himself with the tide and pushes himself forward, slightly downward. For a moment, he wonders how far from home he might be, and though it can't be far he already feels the urge to come up for air. His lungs beg him to do so.

But there is no time. He swims along.

Soon he sees the bottom. Pebbles, unfamiliar plants. A crawfish scurries, startling him. His father had always told him not to be afraid of anything that is smaller than he is, so he reaches out to touch it. It reaches back, extending its tiny claw in solidarity. In his mind, he tells it that he is not to be feared. I am as afraid as you are, he thinks.

His hands graze the bottom. A puff of silt clouds his vision. With confidence, he removes his other hand from his nose and touches the riverbed with both hands. He grabs handfuls of mud and rocks. What a funny feeling, being down here below everything.

The crawfish whispers to him in a secret language only he knows: the bottom is not as low as you can get. You can go further.

So he digs, flinging sand and water plants in every direction. The area around him becomes hazier; there is no way to tell if he is moving at all, but he is certain he is getting closer. By now, his lungs have adjusted; he feels unencumbered by the responsibility to breathe. He digs and digs, never growing weary, creating a small tunnel he could burrow inside. The deeper he ventures, the lighter the sand becomes. Soon, it is weightless. He gathers it by the armful and tosses it behind him.

He can now stand in the tunnel. He is liminal, weightless. A speck of light ahead illuminates the muddy walls, the sandy floor. He runs toward it, not knowing what he is chasing, but believing that it is good.

/SIːDZ/

Ben Egerton

.

that seeds wind-blown or beak-spilled find fissures
that sun-fed and mist-swaddled they cleave solid rock
that granite yields to green
that permanent cedes to the creeping roots of these juvenile upstarts and birds
lodge in the branches and sing

sing

sing

such songs of praise

Our visitors are here. They speak to us in our language and tell us what we already know of our homes, our customs, our gods. They wear our clothes. They talk us into bed and we let them sleep with us, seduced by familiar words on unfamiliar tongues.
Up and awake before the visitors, in the dewy silence of the morning, we try their words for size, like new converts quoting from the minor prophets.

The half-life of faith: Archimedes asked for a long lever, a fulcrum and a place to place it.
Your demand is for something no bigger than a mustard seed: packaged as Semtex,
replacing ball bearings in bullets, as tongues of fire on tribal weddings, substitute
for plutonium to obliterate the gates of paradise.
All along the mountains are not so much as climbed.

That so much has gone to spoil in those idle minutes, that one thing has led to another (a name, a scene, a phrase, a passerby), that momentary opening of the private browser, that brief and unsatisfactory relief, that everything that's sown in the dark will be reaped in the light.

bærlic	hwǣte (white / dazzle)	winberie	ele-bēam	senep-sǣd (synapse / collapse)	fic
barley	wheat	*wineberry*	olive	mustard seed	fig
barely	wait	grape	o live	must seed	fuck
bear me		grave	o love	must-see	
bare me		graven / image			
	weight		o lose	miss me	
bury me	way to go		loss		*fin*

:

I watch you finish clearing the neglect and shit of winter from our raised beds.
You pause, unstoop with hands on hips and the leather loop from the hand fork hooked
over your right index finger. Taking a marker and the small bag of light-white pebbles
you bought before the fall, you write every seed's name on a fresh stone
and push it into the dirt next to each dibbed hole. Not Linnaean or common, for you choose
a new name each spring, each plant.

WAITING ON TRILLIUM

Lisa Muir

I stare at the phone, a land line. It is the current embodiment of my mother, slim and inert. From far away I have called my father. Then my sister. Then my father again. We engage in multiple conversations like this during the day, relaying information. Later, once I arrive, I will stare at my mother, as unresponsive as an idle phone.

My mother has always ended a phone call, "Bysie."

***

My father warns my sister and me. Our mother has been angry that he has not taken her home. She can be totally out of it. He worries she will become willful and a management problem. These words seem so odd from my adoring father, a physician who loves his wife so very much, and who finds it too hard to be on this side of the medical profession. Her upstairs is gone, he tells my sister and me.

***

To come here my parents depart from the same hospital but with differing results. My mother is hustled out of bed, rolled away through the doorway, seemingly disappearing. She is whisked into an ambulance and expediently transferred. My father's departure is delayed by a myriad of interior hallways and a simple but frustrating lack of close parking.

At the check-in desk to this new place my frail mother is asked the year. 2018. She is correct. A few questions later she is asked to name the year again. She replies 1920. My father is still on his way. Without consulting any family member, a DNR bracelet is placed around her thin wrist.

Two hours later they reunite awkwardly, my mother's eyes vacant. Who slapped this DNR bracelet on her, my father demands. Asked once or a hundred times, the answer is the same. A brusque nurse uses the word mistake, but offers no apology. It takes just a moment to make a mistake.

A parking problem could have killed his wife.

In between my mother sleeps.

**

This place has a name. This name is displayed on a newly created sign and includes the major donor's name connected to the words in-patient therapy. It also makes reference to memory and long-term care. The name is far too long to remember. Within my mother's room we use other terms tentatively, like facility and unit and therapy and rehab . . . and simply the place.

**

My mother's surprise at my arrival is real and childlike. She asks where I will sleep and I say the second bedroom. I mean of her house. She is surprised a second bedroom exists. She means next to her room. She asks my sister for a glass of wine. My sister leaves the room and wastes some time meandering hallways. Bysie calls out our mother.

"All out," my sister confesses upon her return.

In between my mother sleeps.

**

Trillium can take seven years to rise and bloom. The seeds are slow to germinate and spread. My mother moves like trillium.

**

But my mother is not a trillium seed. She is eighty-four. It is late morning and my father stands in front of my mother. Seated, she reaches languidly and ineffectively for her walker. She calls it a stroller. It is behind my father. He stands fast, refusing to move. My mother is so angry. My mother does not know she is angry. She asks why he has not come to visit in two days. He reminds her he ate breakfast with her just two hours ago.

The following day she will claim someone stole her walker, but my father has safely stowed it away in the trunk of the car. She will tell me a story of the nurses taking her seventy cents and a box of cookies. She claims her linens brought from home have been replaced with an inferior grade. In between stories she sleeps.

Someone, perhaps a nurse, has provided a distraction. In vivid color the 2018 Winter Olympic Games stream across the TV's screen from the wall across from my mother's bed in the tiny room. Such strong bodies.

No one is watching.

My sister thanks me for all I have done. She directs our mother in a firm voice; our mother, naked and sitting on a toilet seat, complies, roles reversed. This is my mother's version of a shower right now. She sits quietly while we rub her down with wet washcloths.

I have done so little I say. I have only been present.

My sister says softly, yes, you have.

We help my mother back to her Dunning Ultra-Light 2000 Full-Electric Hospital Bed, $1506.67 as advertised on a helpful website. I have looked it up, a kind of test to determine whether we have brought her to the right place. Every one of my mother's moves is painful, arduous, every moment consumed with how to negotiate the next moment. Our mother asks if it is Tuesday. We tell her it is Saturday.

Later that night I will dream that my mother is just eighteen inches tall.

My husband finds a surgical mask and places it over his eyes rather than his mouth, securing the strap at the back of his head. He claims he is a surgeon. To anyone outside my mother's room, outside our circle, outside our family, blinding himself seems irreverent, but it is very funny at the time and what we all need. My mother actually emits a belly laugh.

In between she sleeps.

Trillium can take seven years to rise and bloom. It too has various names: trillium recurvatum, prairie trillium . . . and the bloody butcher.

My mother has a bleed in the brain. It is not called a stroke but it is a kind of stroke. My mother sometimes cannot finish sentences. She begins "The . . ." and does not continue, visibly searching, befuddled, then turning away. Another time my mother speaks words that do not exist. In between she sleeps. *Bysie.*

***

In a lucid moment my mother asks a visiting physician whether she is terminal. He is kind. He smiles and tells her everyone is terminal, that she just has more information than most. My mother does not grasp his humor. She stares out the picture window along the wall beside her bed, detecting a road. That is either Sixteen-Mile Road or Big Beaver, she announces. These are real throughways, but outside Detroit. My mother is in North Carolina. She has lived in North Carolina nearly a decade.

***

My father returns the walker to my mother but she wants to creep to the bathroom without it. It does not work right, she tells us. We don't want you to fall again I say. My mother still has just enough steam to shoot me a glare. I think she calls me a smartass. I am pleased to detect this bit of wit.

I won't fall, she confirms. I don't know if she believes that, wants to believe that, or wants us all to go away.

***

Surprisingly, my mother's dog is allowed in the facility. My father brings him in under his arm. The dog has a terrible cough. The nurses appear at doorways, concerned, but no one asks my father to remove the animal. I do not know whether to be alarmed or grateful. I do not know a lot of things.

***

We find my mother sitting on the edge of her single bed chatting with a nurse. Her legs dangle like a child's They are swollen and seep liquid into her slippers, which are nearly soaked. My mother has actual tiny rivulets running down her calves. She speaks of Rembrandt and a famous self-portrait he painted in 1629 when he was just 22, now referred to as Self-portrait with disheveled hair, she clarifies. She speaks so matter-of-factly. She had seen the portrait at the Rijksmuseum in Amsterdam.

All this she remembers.

Later he would paint himself in his velvet hat, reinvigorating a fifteenth-century sartorial statement out of fashion by the beginning of the seventeenth century, she tells the nurse.

How can she suddenly remember words like sartorial and reinvigorated?

Artists ever afterward adopted the velvet beret she finishes.

The nurse claps. Beatrice! That is so interesting, she says. We are glad to have you here.

Later my father and my sister and I will not be glad to leave her there.

***

Trillium can live for some twenty-five years but are susceptible to forces like deer who browse the colonies, as they are called, weakening their stamina, causing collapse.

***

My mother asks for a tablecloth. The room has no table. My father returns home, and using logic and practicality, selects the top linen from a large stack. My mother is German. My mother hoards anything with a lacey pattern or flowers, especially edelweiss. Walls must be decorated. Shelves must be packed. Floors boast a myriad of rugs. All surfaces must be covered with lively patterns.

I hate that tablecloth, my mother says. It is one she herself embroidered some fifty years ago. After some labored thought my mother admits, I put so much work into it. Then why don't you like it, Mom? I ask. We all wait for my mother to formulate a response, as though she is an oracle.

I just don't.

***

The dog has a growth in its chest that is pushing against its trachea. Surgery could be done but he is dog-elderly. It is the lesser of two evils, letting him deal with the malady that will likely cause him to suffocate at some point, or cut into his dog-ancient form.

My mother has diabetes and liver cancer and faulty bone marrow. The liver cancer requires a stent be replaced in a bile duct every three months. The surgeons do so by going down her throat. A human's mouth is not clean and during one procedure some months ago enough bacteria are taken down with the stent to create a raging infection which overwhelms her body. She nearly dies. In addition, over the past weeks she has fallen and struck her head on the floor twice due to dehydration— and all of the above. Urged to drink more liquids, her sodium count plunges. One solution begets another problem. There is no balance anymore.

My mother used to live for the dog but cares far less now. My father places the dog on the bed next to my mother. She reaches for it vaguely. My father is healthy. He will not die with her; instead, she and the dog are dying together. It seems a strange comfort. They sleep.

***

My mother wakes. We have so much stuff, she says to no one in particular.

Has she dreamed of the house from which she has been removed? Is she making an undetectable request? Is she making a bequest?

***

My father will learn to make eggs for breakfast.

My father will learn to grocery shop beyond picking up a wedge of cheese or a container of detergent for my mother.

My father will learn to do laundry on mom's complicated washer with all its choices. I tell him when in doubt choose "Normal." Can hardly go wrong there.

My father will learn to sweep the floor; he will learn to fold clothes; he will learn where the clean dishes belong in the cupboards—or perhaps he will create a new system.

He asks my sister to help him pick out matching clothes for our mother. She suggests comfortable clothes instead. Dad is a physician but from the generation when duties were segregated.

***

Trillium seedlings lay in the dark, underground for a year or more. They will seem incapable, unresponsive. They sleep. Then one will send a green leaf up to find the light. Perhaps a few, or even a group, will follow.

Trillium can take a full seven years to rise and bloom. Unaware of past or present or future, or of its own patience, it waits. Dozens, or maybe thousands, or maybe millions of seeds will be lost—yet joy will be found in the few flickers of green. To the rest, *Bysie*.

THE FIRST MULBERRY

Laurel Eshelman

has dropped.

On the path
not yet blackened by blood and seed,
a lone ant circles round the sapphire.
Like Aaron measuring Moses' ascent
it hesitates at jewel's edge,
antennae flush
and scissored jaws flexing,
then hurries away
to fly wing
and dry crumb.

THE VIEWING

Courtney O'Banion Smith

WHITE OAK, Miocene Epoch
Houston Museum of Natural Science

It took twenty million years to get here:
shiny cross-section of petrified white oak—
disk displayed as lighted evidence of the death
of my grandfather more than thirty years ago.

The pale wood turned smooth black stone of filigreed rings,
spiderweb-thin grooves that filtered oxygen for generations
bisected by a tube of white *where ground water*
brought in oxygen and bleached away the dark cellulose
present in the mineralized wood: a trachea
whose blackened lobes inhaled smoke instead of air.

My father's father rolled cigarettes
in a green tin lawn chair on his front porch,
knees crossed in polyester kakis. King Edward VII
watched over the loose molasses-smelling tobacco
from the underside of the lid-flap
of the yellow cardboard cigar box.
The pink tip of Grandpa's tongue
dampened the edge of the thin white paper translucent.
Yellowed, thick fingers and fingernails
delicately picked off flecks of tobacco as he spat.
The strike, the flair, the sharp sulfur odor
commingled with the sweet exhalation of white smoke
drifting between chipped white columns.

I was seven but not the youngest
when the family gathered inside his white wooden house.
Grandma's wails overtook the quieter
crying of his grown children that first woke me.
I was led in to see the shell he had left of himself.
Brown and yellow striped curtains.

Soft white glow of a lacy lampshade.
My little brain couldn't contain
the entire scene. I looked for it,
but his tongue was lost
in the blackness of his gaping mouth.

Even at seven, I was offended by
the tasteful artifice of the dead:
Mouth closed. Skin pinkened
for display. Face swollen
behind pointless square glasses over
sunken eyelids. Fingers and nails
now caked in flesh-toned makeup
folded gently at the waist in affected repose.

Standing in the museum's darkened room
filled with roundish slabs lit by spotlights,
I can see some beauty in it now.
They lived once and continue to matter,
although in an altered state—
imposed memories, a satisfying obsequy
for those left behind—
even if only for a moment,
to viewers filing past one at a time.

PURE SPECULATION

Jim Richards

Relief from suffering might be finding its way across an ocean on a raft with a makeshift sail. Or perhaps a rogue tendril of joy will be discovered breaking through the earth beside a sprig of wild peppermint. Likewise, that tingling between your ribs is possibly pain growing an arm to drag itself away. And when the night clears, maybe grief will sleep alone under the stars, and wolves will devour it. All in all, if hope ever arrives to embrace us, she should not be surprised when we hold her at bay, and say: *explain.*

A REVIEW OF JESSIE VAN EERDEN'S *THE LONG WEEPING: PORTRAIT ESSAYS*

Christie Purifoy

The boundaries of creative nonfiction will always be as fluid as water.
—Mary Clearman Blew

In a portrait, you have room to have a point of view. The image may not be literally what's going on, but it's representative.
—Annie Leibovitz

Ours has been called the age of literary memoir. Though I roll my eyes at grandiose words like *age*—predictably so since ours is also, we are told, an age of irony—I am convinced there is substance to this claim. Memoir, and its umbrella category *creative nonfiction*, belongs to us in the way the doorstop novel belonged to the Victorians. The significance of the innovative writing that has emerged for decades from within this general category has been proved by a proliferation of labels: not only *memoir*, *literary memoir*, and *creative nonfiction*, but also *narrative journalism, narrative nonfiction, literary nonfiction*, and *personal essay*. It is as if traditional terms of literary description burst at the seams when applied to the best new nonfiction writing. Nowhere is this pressure more evident than in that overlooked but absolutely necessary device, the subtitle.

Of course, if subtitles are overlooked, they are only overlooked in a scholarly sense. Subtitles are not given much critical attention because scholars and reviewers understand they are not an intrinsic element of a literary work of art. They are too often shaped by a publisher's or a marketer's whim, and who can say if a particular subtitle was agreeable to the writer at all? Yet writers and readers know how much a subtitle matters and also how much more it matters in the wide-ranging realm of creative nonfiction.

When I wrote a book my editor privately called *memoir-ish* the only delay in the publication process involved the subtitle. Everyone involved in choosing it understood that in a shifting sea of new nonfiction work the subtitle is one of the most important signals guiding a reader's expectations. We disagreed over the subtitle because it wasn't easy for a handful of words to do as much work as we needed them to do.

If subtitles for nonfiction books are beacons in a wild and varied terrain, then the subtitle of Jessie Van Eerden's new book casts an especially bright and exact beam: *The Long Weeping* is, we read on the cover, a collection of "Portrait Essays."

***

The Victorians had their portrait novels (Henry James's *Portrait of a Lady* comes first to mind) and now Van Eerden gives us the contemporary equivalent, a collection of portrait essays. And though writing an essay-long character description might be an assignment in any creative writing class, Van Eerden's collection both fulfills and explodes the expectations established by those combined words *portrait* and *essay*. By the end of this book, I couldn't even say with confidence whether I had read a work of nonfiction or fiction, suggesting that our literary moment might best be captured in the tension of oppositional pairs like fiction/nonfiction, short story/essay, and memoir/anti-memoir, that final pair the preferred category of a similar, genre-defying contemporary writer, Rebecca Solnit.

Van Eerden's creations are fiction and nonfiction, portraits and self-portraits, stories and essays, all. But these elements don't add up to chaos or even collage but to a shimmering and much more seamless whole. These various forms, as antithetical as they might at first seem to minds like ours used to analyzing and categorizing, don't function as separate entities or diminish one another, and it isn't merely that they complement one another (though they do). Rather, Van Eerden's careful nonfiction and honest memoir build toward a final exuberant portrait that blends both of these elements with history, religion, and imagination in a work of literary portraiture that is both dazzling yet also painfully precise.

By the end of *The Long Weeping*, we discover that Van Eerden has shattered yet another boundary within the contemporary literary scene and proven false one of our most persistent artistic myths: that one cannot create serious art and also take seriously the culture and spirituality of traditional religion.

***

The Long Weeping begins with self-portrait. This is an astute choice because it suggests that this portrait artist is willing to turn her searching eye on her own self as well as on others, a willingness that matters when the art in question is so full of hazards and snares. The most important questions invoked in the early essays are questions about the ethics of portraiture and the complicated power dynamics between artists and their subjects. Is it possible to see others whole? Can we communicate what we see in ways that are not reductive? Van Eerden, at least early in the book, seems unsure and her descriptions of an elderly neighbor she knew as a child in West Virginia are deliberately circumspect. It's a measure of Van Eerden's ability that circumspect in these essays never means vague or imprecise.

Van Eerden tells us that this neighbor once "looked at the camera dead center" when "President Johnson's photographers came combing through Appalachia in the Sixties," but the camera captured only the ugly traces of poverty and none of the dignity or love. This essay, then, aims to show "Eliza" whole, a project that is as much about the writer as it is the woman being written about. Van Eerden never claims that this reparative project will matter to one who "never saw [herself] in the way they saw you, framed and cropped for a project," but it seems to matter a great deal to the writer. Biography melds with autobiography, and a true portrait of "Eliza" begins to seem like a necessary and even foundational element of Van Eerden's attempt to describe her family home and, by extension, to tell her own story.

If the epigraph from Kafka is to be believed, this attempt is also a significant one for Van Eerden's readers: "We photograph things in order to drive them out of our minds," Kafka writes. This whole book can be seen as an attempt to invite others in through something we might call anti-photography. Anti-photographic portraits welcome even "othered" parts of the self, such as the body parts we prefer to hide, and even "othered" aspects of life, such as failure, sorrow, and death. Van Eerden's portrait essays are radically hospitable.

***

Many of these things we prefer not to see are present in the autobiographical prologue, but they belong to the whole community: the young narrator has hairy legs, her teenaged sister has itchy armpits, and the old people in the church funeral service have grinding hips and blue-veined skin. It is right that the body would figure so largely in a collection of portraits, yet Van Eerden seems to describe bodies in a way that goes beyond the portraitist's usual mandate to portray through the physical something of what lies beneath superficial physical traits. Over the course of this collection, faithful attention to the uniqueness of bodies is precisely what allows Van Eerden to explore the spiritual concerns that are shared by everybody.

In the prologue, a young Van Eerden flees death, in the form of a funeral, in jelly shoes that pinch. She drinks deeply from a hand pump in a scene that seems to deliberately recall Jesus offering living water to the woman at the well. This self-portrait is followed by portraits of others who shared Van Eerden's mountain home, among them family, friends, neighbors, as well as Christian mystics and Biblical figures who also seem right at home in the West Virginia mountains. By the book's end a Biblical Rizpah, who is also in some ways a self-portrait of an older Van Eerden matured and even blessed by sorrow, refuses to flee. She lies down with death and receives something better than a miracle, not the reversal of death but something beyond it.

In an essay concerned with the writing process, Van Eerden affirms her commitment "to say things true," but she clarifies: "And by true I mean, not factual, but honest." Van Eerden's portrait of Rizpah, whose story is little more than a footnote in the second book of Samuel, is flagrantly and riotously non-factual. Rizpah keeps her vigil over the bodies of her sons and grandsons along a highway, is fed by a shoplifting Kroger employee, and dons a wild pink wig. I hate to use a reviewer's cliché for such an astonishing piece of writing, but every cliché was once a useful phrase and Van Eerden's portrayal of Rizpah is, I am sure, an artistic and spiritual tour de force.

***

If *The Long Weeping* teases out the possibilities of oppositional pairings like biography/autobiography and fiction/nonfiction it suggests, to me, another meaningful pairing: portrait/anti-portrait. With a nod to Solnit's conception of the anti-memoir, a form that allows for the difficulty in knowing the self, the portrait/anti-portrait line does not hinge on the difference between a portrait and a self-portrait. I was convinced only a few pages into *The Long Weeping* that portraits and self-portraits lie right alongside one another on a continuum, and the two weave in and out of one another in these essays. Rather by portrait/anti-portrait I mean to describe the most subtle portrait offered in this book: God's portrait.

A portrait of God by an atheist would portray absence. A portrait of God by a believer would emphasize presence. Van Eerden's anti-portrait offers something between the two: a portrait of God as most present in absence. In the "droughted" world of *The Long Weeping*, a world that includes Appalachia and ancient Israel, we pray for rain, but we can find God neither in the rain nor its lack. The problem with rain is that it does not remember—as memoir remembers—but wipes the past, and especially its grief, "clean and clear." The problem with rain is that it "does not penetrate, it is too hard and too fast." Instead, Van Eerden's God is found in "tears" and in the morning "dew." This is "the quench within the thirst itself." God's is the presence that surprises us among "rubbish" and within "ash-heap[s]."

In her portrait of thirteenth-century Beguine mystics, Van Eerden tells us, "The way I see it, a mystic takes a peek at God and then does her best to show the rest of us what she saw. She'll use image-language, not discourse." Van Eerden makes no claim to have seen God, but the God she can't quite see is everywhere in these portraits: "Sometimes you see nothing in the sky, no promises or marks of Jesus's feet, no sign that he's coming back to bring you home-so you write the nothing and the no-place, too."

In *The Long Weeping*, questions about the ethics of portraiture become questions about the spirituality of portraiture. Is it possible to see God and to see God whole? Is it possible to communicate what we see in ways that are not reductive? Van Eerden seems consistently unsure. In the final pages, Rizpah describes God as "beneath God—like a seed in a covered furrow," but admits "she doesn't really know." Yet this reader is convinced. The most successful though perhaps least accessible portrait in *The Long Weeping* is a portrait of a God who is found in the places we would least expect to find God, the very places where God seems most *not* to be. "I have always wanted to know if you can love emptiness," Van Eerden writes. In this beautiful, startling book I glimpsed the possibility, not only of loving emptiness, but of being loved by it, too.

Made in the USA
Monee, IL
25 February 2022

91870011R00083